Y0-BZK-439

Comprehensive Character-Building Classroom

A Handbook For Teachers

Other Books by Dr. Lori Wiley
Comprehensive Character-Building Classroom Workbook
Comprehensive Character-Building Classroom Assessment Kit
Comprehensive Character-Building School
Comprehensive Character-Building College

Comprehensive Character-Building Classroom

A Handbook For Teachers

Lori Sandford Wiley, Ph.D.

LONGWOOD COMMUNICATIONS

Copyright © 1998 by Lori Sandford Wiley. *Third Printing, 1998, revised edition.* Printed in the United States of America.

ISBN: 1-883928-27-3

Library of Congress Catalog Card Number: 98-84020

All rights reserved. No part of this book may be reproduced or transmitted in any form or by any means, electronic or mechanical, including photocopying, recording, or by any information storage and retrieval system without written permission from the author. Fair Use is allowed for teachers in their own classrooms.

Published by:

Longwood Communications
397 Kingslake Drive
DeBary, FL 32713

For more information contact:

Character Development Foundation
P.O. Box 4782
Manchester, NH 03108-4782
(603)472-3063 telephone and fax
character@juno.com

Warning - Disclaimer

This book is designed to provide information in regard to the subject matter covered. It is sold with the understanding that the publisher and author are not engaged in rendering legal or accounting services. If legal assistance is required, the services of a competent attorney should be sought. It is not the purpose of this manual to reprint all the information that is otherwise available to the author and/or publisher, but to complement, amplify and supplement other texts. You are urged to read all the available material, learn as much as possible about character education and to tailor the information to your individual needs. For more information, see the many resources in the reference list at the end of this book. Every effort has been made to make this manual as complete and as accurate as possible. However, there may be mistakes both typographical and in content. Therefore, this text should be used only as a general guide and not as the ultimate source of writing/publishing information. Furthermore, this manual contains information made available only up to the printing date. The purpose of this manual is to educate. The author and publisher shall have neither liability nor responsibility to any person or entity with respect to any loss or damage caused, or alleged to be caused, directly or indirectly by the information contained in this book. If you do not wish to be bound by the above, you may return this book to the publisher for a full refund.

© Jeff Greenberg/Visuals Unlimited (girl drawing, students talking)
© Bernd Wittich/Visuals Unlimited (children in sandbox)

Acknowledgments
to

Tom Lickona, mentor and friend

William Kilpatrick, my dissertation director at
Boston College

Lloyd Wiley, my husband and best friend

Madonna Murphy, a true character educator

all the New Hampshire teachers who took workshops with
me and shared their ideas

and

Board Members
of
the Character Development Foundation

Table of Contents

Introduction

I began collecting information for this book as part of a doctoral dissertation on character education. The first two chapters provide the general background and a brief theoretical orientation from research. The first chapter explains and defines what is meant by character, why it is important, and how it is acquired. It presents both psychological and philosophical points of view. The second chapter explains what character education is and why it is needed in schools today.

LC5

In my work with classroom teachers I asked them how they taught character, what methods they used. After having collected ideas from thousands of teachers, I have organized six categories, which, I believe, encompass all aspects of a comprehensive character-building classroom. These six categories can be called the LC5 model. L stands for moral leadership. The five Cs are as follows: climate, community, correction, curriculum and common projects.

There are six chapters, one for each of these six categories. These chapters describe the components of a comprehensive character-building classroom: **moral leadership, moral climate, moral community, moral correction,** a **moral curriculum,** and **class projects**.

The first category is **moral leadership**. The teacher serves as a model for students to emulate. In order to teach character education, educators must be people of high moral character. This chapter describes in detail many ethical issues faced by educators.

The second category is **moral climate**, sometimes called *ethos* or *environment*. Classroom climate is the most pervasive and far reaching aspect of any character education program. It is the first thing noticed and the last thing remembered. Climate may be described as what is seen, heard, and felt. This chapter describes how to bring a sense of excitement to character education through a campaign. Campaigning is a planned and orderly way of building student motivation to acquire good character.

The third category is **moral community**, sometimes referred to as *structure, governance,* or *classroom management.* This describes how the classroom is run, its mode of operation. Who is in charge of what? How is it organized? How do students take responsibility?

The fourth category is **moral correction**, commonly called *behavior management, positive guidance* or *discipline.* Character education is used to correct misbehavior. Rather than change or modify behavior alone, the character which produces the behavior is addressed.

The fifth category is **moral curriculum**. Character education can be included both through content (what is taught) and process (how it is taught). It may be a subject in itself such as a course in ethics or moral education, but it should be part of every academic discipline, lesson plan, and activity. A thematic approach is described.

The sixth category is **class projects** or **community service learning**. As students adopt projects to make the world a better place, they are making themselves better people.

I believe that all classroom efforts to educate for character fall into one of these categories, so a chapter is devoted to each. The last chapter describes methods of assessing the character of students, as well as a character education program. The intent of this book is to provide tools for teachers who wish to implement a comprehensive character-building classroom.

CHAPTER 1

Character

WHAT IT IS

Character is a reliable inner disposition to act in a morally good way, having qualities such as honesty and integrity. It refers to the ethical standards that make up the inner nature of a person (*Webster's New Collegiate Dictionary*, 1980). *Character* can also be used more broadly to define what kind of person one is, whether good or bad.

In the 1960s and '70s, psychology focused primarily on behavior, without recognizing that an inner nature existed. Attempting to deal with behavior was like the rug merchant whose carpet had a large bump in it. According to the Chinese proverb, when he stepped on the bump to flatten it out, the bump reappeared in a new spot. He jumped on the bump again, and it disappeared briefly but emerged once more in a new place. Again and again he jumped, until finally he lifted one corner of the carpet and an angry snake slithered out. Addressing behaviors or misbehaviors does not get at the central issue: the character of the person choosing these behaviors.

Character is shown through patterns of behavior, often called *habits*, as described in the following:

A Gentleman once advertised for a boy to assist him in his office. Nearly fifty applied for the place. Out of the whole number he in a short time chose one, and sent all the rest away. "I should like to know," said a friend who was present, "on what ground you chose that boy. He had not one recommendation with him."

"You are mistaken," said the gentleman; "he had a great many: He wiped his shoes when he came in, and closed the door after him, showing that he was tidy and orderly. He gave up his seat instantly to that lame man, showing that he was kind and thoughtful. He took off his cap when he came in, and answered my questions promptly and respectfully, showing that he was polite. He lifted up the book which I had purposely laid on the floor, and placed it on the table, while all the rest stepped over it or shoved it aside, showing that he was careful. And he waited quietly for his turn instead of pushing the others aside, showing that he was modest. When I talked with him I noticed that his clothes were carefully brushed, his hair was in nice order... Don't you call these things letters of recommendation? I do, and what I can tell about a boy by using my eyes for ten minutes is worth more than all the fine letters he can bring me" (Appleton, 1884).

WHY CHARACTER IS IMPORTANT

Most people want to be good, or at least they want to be around people who are good. Everyone wants a friend, spouse, teacher, or parent who is honest, dependable, loving, kind, and trustworthy. Teachers and parents want students to show these qualities. The American dream for most is not to be rich or famous, but to be happy and satisfied with life. Satisfaction comes from choosing what is right and doing one's best to make the world a better place. Americans who followed this dream became the "salt of the earth," the preservatives of our society. Throughout history there have been moral people who took responsibility, cared for their families and others, showed up to work on time, and were conscientious in performing menial tasks well. We recognize the benefits good character brings to society. Thomas Jefferson believed a democracy and freedom depended on having citizens of good character. On the other hand, bad character causes a breakdown of society, and we all pay in many ways, through prison costs if nothing else. Good character is a necessity and an asset to society. Society needs good people (Kennedy, 1994).

HOW CHARACTER IS ACQUIRED

There are many theories regarding how character is acquired (Lickona, 1976). The premise of this book is that, although there may be genetic predispositions and certainly there are environmental influences, **character is internally controlled by each individual through personal choice, goal setting, decision making, and habits of daily life.** In the movie *Trading Places*, two stockbrokers place a dollar bet on whether economic standing can change a rogue into a good person and a well-bred person into a rogue. It reminds me of the college professor who told me that the only reason he does not steal is because he gets a paycheck. He grew up in the ghettos lying, stealing and cheating for survival and believes honesty is a function of socioeconomic status. However, I grew up in a wealthy town where there are frequent reports of fraud and embezzlement. White collar neighborhoods produce their own white collar crimes and corruption. I do not believe morality is a function of socioeconomic status. Each person, regardless of socioeconomic status, makes moral choices.

Teachers who believe this organize their classrooms so that students are taking responsibility for their own actions, making choices, participating in decision making, solving problems, planning, and evaluating themselves.

Through Thinking: Information Processing

Information processing theorists believe that behavior is controlled by thought, that knowing motivates doing, and that specific cognitive skills must be mastered in order to exhibit good moral behavior (Camp & Bash, 1985; Shure, 1989; Meichenbaum, 1977). They use a systematic approach of task analysis, identifying subskills, and finding strategies to master them. The sub-skills include problem solving, predicting consequences, reading the feelings of others, and planning. Decision making is referred to as the executive function of cognition. It is used for self-control, self-management, self-regulation, goal setting, and planning.

Children are beginners or *novices* in using these skills, but with practice, they can reach the status of *expert*. They learn to restructure their thinking and thus change or improve their behavior. They are taught to think out loud, using language as a self-regulator (Vygotsky, 1934). Resisting temptation and delaying gratification have been successfully taught using this approach.

Teachers who use this approach teach students the steps of problem solving and planning (Crary, 1984). Goal setting, planning, self-management, and self-regulation are built into the curriculum (Mannix, 1989).

Through Empathic Feelings

Empathy is a motivating force for developing moral behavior (Damon, 1988; Eisenberg & Miller, 1987; Oliner & Oliner, 1988). Empathy is the ability to detect, understand, and identify with the feelings of others. It includes perspective taking, being able to predict how another person thinks and feels, reading expressions, gestures, words, and actions. As children are exposed to a wide range of feelings and learn to accurately interpret the feelings of others, they increase in moral behavior (Santrock & Yussen, 1988). Carol Gilligan (1982), Nel Noddings (1984), and Mary Brabeck (1989) believe there are gender differences in moral thinking, that females tend to be more empathic and focused on interpersonal aspects of morality.

Since empathy is important to character development, teachers encourage students to express their feelings and read the feelings of others. Social interaction in the classroom becomes a teaching tool for building empathy. When one student is sick, upset, or in pain, others are helped to respond in an empathic manner.

Through Beliefs and Vision

Character comes from beliefs, vision, and conscience (Hauerwas, 1983; MacIntyre, 1984). (See diagram.)

A Schematic Mapping of Character Formation

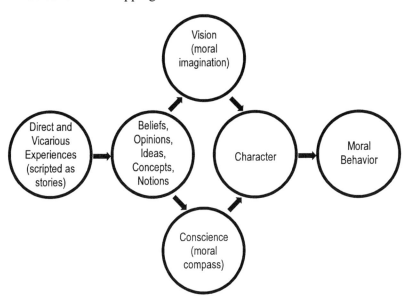

Direct Experiences

In infancy and toddlerhood children are constantly testing ideas by trying a wide variety of behaviors and watching to see what happens. Through trial and error they learn the consequences when they bite, hit, take something away from someone else, use bad words, or destroy property. Two year olds are moral experimenters. They are constantly testing to find out what is acceptable and what is not. They may try the same behaviors over and over again to find out if the results are always the same (Fraiberg, 1959). Reprimands and consistent consequences become internalized as moral rules and concepts.

Moral Leadership

Children also learn from vicarious experiences by watching and imitating what they see or hear. This is called *observational learning* or *imitative learning* (Bandura, 1971). Children are especially imitative of people whom they admire or identify with.

The people who influence them the most are parents. Freud believed the conscience, or super ego, is formed through trying to act like or identify with one's same sex parent (Rieff, 1959). *Parenting styles* have been correlated with character (Baumrind, 1971; Hoffman, 1963; 1975; Zahn-Waxler & Radkey-Yarrow, 1979). A family atmosphere of affection, gentleness, firmness, high moral standards, avoiding harsh punishment, taking an empathic outlook, and using apologies tends to influence children's character positively (Oliner & Oliner, 1988).

Peer groups exert a strong influence toward imitation and conformity, especially as children grow older and desire independence from parents. Teachers, neighbors, and other community members contribute to imitative learning. Teachers who maintain high ethical standards are teaching by example. The media, through advertising and other marketing strategies, use observational learning to influence the values of young people. Stories, books, movies, and television shows profoundly affect character (Kilpatrick, 1986, 1992). Robert Coles in *The call of stories* (1989) wrote that the conscience is formed by remembered voices of the characters in stories, that they become embedded in the conscience of the reader or listener and become guides regarding moral issues. As books and movies are chosen carefully, they have a positive effect on character development.

Story Form and Scripts

Both a dog and a person can experience the same situation. A person puts the experience into a meaningful form such as a story or script which is stored in the memory and produces ideas or concepts. Teachers help students make sense of their experiences by developing their use of the story form. From stories come beliefs and concepts.

Beliefs, Opinions, Concepts, Ideas, Notions, Rules

Information enters the brain where the mind then forms ideas such as "It's wrong to hurt others. Don't take things that don't belong to you. Take care of property. Tell the truth." Children begin to have *ideas* about right and wrong at very early ages (Nucci, 1989). This does not mean they always *do* what is right, or that the conscience controls their behavior, but they begin to have the cognitive structures to know right from wrong. For example, they may show a guilty look but continue with the behavior.

Vision or Moral Imagination

Vision is one's ideals and worldview. It comes from direct experiences, observation, examples, images, stories, books, beliefs, inner monologues, and religious affirmations. When Martin Luther King gave the famous speech, "I Have a Dream," he was referring to vision. Vision energizes and motivates moral behavior. Hauerwas wrote, "moral behavior is an affair, not primarily of choice, but of vision.... The moral life is a struggle and training in how to see" (Hauerwas, 1974, p.20). "Ethics is not just a matter of decisions about specific actions but a way of seeing the world" (Hauerwas, 1974, p.116).

Clarifying one's vision requires using the moral imagination to see beyond "what is" to "what should be." While psychology may describe and explain how humans *do* behave, vision describes how they *should* behave. It provides ideals toward which to strive. Benjamin Mays said,
"It must be born in mind that the tragedy in life doesn't lie in not reaching your goal. The tragedy lies in having no goals to reach. It isn't a calamity to die with dreams unfulfilled, but it is a calamity not to dream. It is not a disaster to be unable to capture your ideal, but it is a disaster to have no ideal to capture. It is not a disgrace not to reach the stars, but it is a disgrace to have no stars to reach for. Not failure, but low aim is sin."
Debby Boone's children's book, *The snow angel* (1991) begins and ends like this:

Rose was a little girl whose eyes were full of dreams. Most people see things just as they are. Rose saw everything blanketed in dreams of what could be. The world was much more beautiful because of it. Rose lived in a village where people had little by little forgotten how to dream. It's not that they meant to. It's just that simple problems seemed to get so big that they couldn't see beyond them. Nothing much seemed to matter anymore, and folks were just trying to make it from one day to the next... Grandfather came to live with them and he talked about the things that could be. He had given her the gift of dreaming... One day he took her to a clearing in the woods, knelt down and pulled a tiny seed out of his coat pocket.

"This is a giant fir tree!" he announced.

"That sure doesn't look like a giant fir tree," one of the children exclaimed.

"Oh, but it is," Grandfather replied. "You just can't see it yet." Then he said, "Dreams are the seeds of change. Nothing grows without a seed... and nothing ever changes without a dream."

Dreams make use of the moral imagination, helping children develop ideas of what could and should be. Ideas become ideals, which change their lives and behavior. There is a proverb which says, "Where there is no vision, the people are unrestrained" (Proverbs 29.18). Self-control comes from vision.

Educators have been accused of chopping learning into tiny pieces called objectives and lesson plans. Unfortunately those little pieces are often meaningless and irrelevant. Time needs to be spent helping students develop their vision and showing them how what they are doing in school fits their vision. Developing student's vision means giving them time to ponder the important things of life, to think profound thoughts about what could and should be.

Conscience

Conscience is that inner light which indicates the right things to do. Like Jiminy Cricket in Pinocchio, the conscience monitors thoughts and behavior in the area of right and wrong. It serves as a moral compass, pointing us in the right direction. Vision provides direction through goals and ideals; the conscience keeps a person on the path. Teachers can help students be aware of their consciences, encouraging them to be sensitive to this moral guide.

Moral Behavior

Character, in turn, is manifest through behavior or action. The behavior we want our students to show is a product of good character.

The Development of Character

Character is formed gradually throughout the lifespan. It continues to be formed in adulthood, even in older people. As Eleanor Roosevelt said, "Character building begins in our infancy, and continues until death." It is not fully formed before birth, during early childhood, in a day, in a year, or in a decade. Unfortunately it is not a stable trait (Hartshorne & May, 1928, 1930). A child may be very good in kindergarten but get into trouble in junior high.

Character develops through the interaction of biological maturation (an innate sense of right and wrong as documented by Nucci, 1989) with experiences, ideals, conscience, completion of developmental tasks, and choices.

Stage theory helps us understand the developmental underpinnings of mature moral judgment. We are better able to scaffold the environment so as to support development when we understand the stage a child is in and anticipate the next.

Psychosocial development

Erikson (1950) identified developmental tasks for each stage of development. The first is **attachment** and a sense of belonging. Veroff and Veroff (1980) state that acceptance is a prerequisite to concern for others. Children need warm, positive relationships in order to develop morally. The deviant behavior of psychopaths and sociopaths is often related to a lack of normal attachments during infancy. Many were abused and neglected. Attachment, acceptance, love, and a sense of belonging continue as human needs throughout life. Teachers find ways to meet these needs in the classroom.

The second developmental task Erikson identified was **autonomy**, a need to show power and control. Autonomy is the developmental task of toddlers, but it is also a fundamental need of all ages. Teachers look for ways to empower students and encourage their decision making. The developmental task for preschoolers is to take **initiative**, and elementary school children have a need for **industry**. The need for involvement and being able to contribute to the group is a lifelong basic need.

Erikson believed the developmental task for adolescents was forming an **identity**. He also believed the search for identity is a lifelong task since one's identity is redefined at different periods of life. Identity, or self image, has a critical role to play in moral development (Berkowitz, 1995). If Jim sees himself as a good person, he will work to bring his actions in line with his identity. "But I don't steal. I'm not a cheater. I'm not like that. That's not me. I don't do things like that," are common remarks by people who are struggling with disparity between alleged action and identity. Reputation is one's identity as perceived by others, usually established by patterns of behavior. Reputation describes expected future actions, based on past experience: "If she was caught stealing, she is a thief and I expect her to steal, so I will be watching her and my pocketbook. If anything is missing, she probably stole it." "I know he is honest because he returned my money to me. I would trust him with my money again." These are the kinds of statements that show how people make predictions and decisions based on reputation.

Erikson believed the developmental task of young adulthood is **intimacy**, having a close friendship or sexual relationship. Friendship-building in school prepares students for this important part of moral development.

The developmental task in middle adulthood is **generativity**, being involved in community, family and occupation. Through character education students become involved in community service learning.

The last task he identified was **integrity**, a stage in older adulthood. In this stage they question their value to society. Each of the stages presents a developmental task that is important in character development.

Cognitive Development

Jean Piaget (1932) and Lawrence Kohlberg (1981) found that children go through qualitatively different stages of moral reasoning (Lickona, 1993). In *The moral judgment of the child,* Piaget described stages through which children pass. He believed that toddlers and preschool children are pre-moral. When they begin to show moral thinking, they enter Stage One, called Moral Reasoning or Heteronomous Morality.

Stage One: **Moral Realism or Heteronomous Morality** (elementary school): In this stage children have a clear sense of right and wrong. They often believe there is one right answer to every situation. They trust adults and do not question their moral judgments. ("The teacher says...") There is a strong need for rules, which are seen as immutable, unchanging, and to be blindly obeyed. Children think in terms of moral absolutes. They believe in **immanent justice**, that if they break a rule they will automatically be punished, perhaps by slipping on a banana peel or being struck by a bolt of lightning. They also display **realistic thinking**, believing that all external reality is related to their own thoughts and experiences. For example, if they slip and fall, it is because they did something wrong and are being punished. In Stage One, they are **egocentric**, meaning they can only see a situation from their own point of view. They see situations in terms of what they want and feel. They also think in terms of **objective responsibility**, meaning right and wrong are determined by the **result**, rather than **intention**. Here is a vignette for testing this concept:

Mary was trying to help her mother sew and accidentally cut a huge hole in the apron they were making. Jane decided to play with the scissors her mother had told her not to touch. She slipped and cut a small hole in her apron. Which girl's action was worse?

Young children tend to look at the size of the hole, while older children look at the intention of the person.

Stage Two: **Morality of Reciprocity or Autonomous Morality**: In Stage Two, previous thought patterns disappear, to be replaced with logic. Children begin to understand that rules are formed through agreement and negotiation. Rules can be questioned and changed. In this stage children become believers in equalitarianism, or equal justice, rather than egocentrism, because they can now see things from another person's point of view. They can accept the concept of fairness for everybody. They are able to hold more than one right answer in their minds. They look at the intent behind the act. They believe that the punishment should be restitution rather than some unrelated "act of God." They set up hypothetical moral dilemmas and enjoy discussing more than one possible solution.

A Stage One thinker would accept an adult's explanation. A Stage Two thinker now uses logic and hypothesizes to explore various logical points of view. Stage Two thinkers may seem to have lost a sense of absolutes as they reason. They can find logical explanations to justify wrongful actions.

Stage Three: **Mature Adult Thinking:** Piaget had begun to develop a third stage, unnamed, where the ethics of cooperation, social-moral complexities and moral ideals are better understood.

Adults weave a complex web of moral concerns, all of which are inter-related. Moral decisions are constantly re-evaluated, and flexible thinking is essential.

In Stage Three dozens of interrelated moral issues are addressed through practical, everyday decision making. There are constant adjustments, negotiations, and evaluations (Is my plan working? Is everyone happy? Am I doing the right thing?).

Piaget and Kohlberg did not expect moral reasoning to be taught. They believed that children's moral reasoning would develop when they were exposed to social interaction, role playing, conflicts, differences of opinion, dilemmas, and discussion. As students listen to different points of view, clarify their own thoughts and misconceptions, generate and evaluate ideas, and engage in social perspective-taking by examining the feelings of others, they develop moral reasoning. The teacher should create cognitive conflict or dissonance by calling attention to discrepancies, contradictions, and inconsistencies. Other teaching techniques include posing questions, encouraging critical thinking, and keeping a supportive atmosphere in which students become aware of moral issues in daily life and examine their own beliefs.

Because the child's mind is actively constructing knowledge, the teacher is not so much providing answers as material, experiences, and high-level questions to engage the child's thinking. According to Hohmann, Banet, & Weikert (1979), "active learning, the direct and immediate experiencing of objects, people and events, is a necessary condition for cognitive restructuring. Young children learn concepts through self-initiated activity. Learning is decisive and lasting to the degree that it is active and direct" (p. 3). Using this approach, adults give opportunities for students to form their own ideas through discovery. Teachers do not *tell* the *right* answer, but help students discover it.

Kohlberg (see chapter 6) built on Piagetian theory and re-defined the stages of moral reasoning.

Summary

Character is acquired in many ways. While there may be genetic predispositions toward both good and bad behavior, each person has the power of choice and self-control. Character development includes thinking and empathy. It is formed by experiences, observation, beliefs, vision, conscience, decision-making, behavior, and habits. Character is formed over time and across the lifespan. According to Erikson, there are developmental tasks for each stage of life. The accomplishment of these tasks forms character. Piaget and Kohlberg examined the development of moral reasoning.

Exercises

Answer the following:

1. *How do you think character is formed? What has influenced your character?*
2. *Describe one experience you had in which you learned a moral lesson.*
3. *Describe one person who made a difference in your life.*
4. *What are your ideals? What is your vision for yourself? What kind of person do you want to be? What part do you want to play in this world? Where do you get your vision?*
5. *How did your parents influence your character?*
6. *How did your peers influence you to make moral or immoral decisions?*
7. *Describe a moral choice you had to make and what went through your mind.*
8. *Describe yourself morally: What is your moral identity?*
9. *What stage do you think you are in (Erikson and Piaget)? What developmental task are you facing right now, and how is it shaping your character?*
10. *Describe, design, or draw the ideal school, teacher, principal, students, community, government, or world.*

Exercises for the Classroom

11. *Role play:*
    You are principal this year. How should you run the school?
    You are the teacher this year. How should the classroom be run?
    You are serving on a school improvement task force. Work together to redesign this school. Take a walk around the school to help give you ideas. (A cooperative learning exercise.)
12. *Assign community roles (banker, lawyer, store owner, restaurateur, gas station attendant, doctor, etc.) and form a task force to create an ideal community. (cooperative learning exercise.)*
13. *One way to develop vision is to encourage students to have heroes*

and heroines, people who portray desired ideals. Every culture has heroes and heroines, who exemplify the ideals of that culture. Children, as well as adults, have a psychological need for heroes and heroines, people whom they admire and want to emulate. Heroes and heroines are chosen based on a person's ideals. In American culture the heroes and heroines are usually rock stars, professional athletes, or movie stars. For doing a unit on heroes and heroines, see Chapter 7.

14. Role play the following case studies and discuss your answer:

Case study 1

Teacher: Isn't their character already formed before they come to school?

Case study 2

Parent 1: Is character genetic? Are they born with it?

Case study 3

Parent 2: Are there children who will never have a conscience or sense of right and wrong?

Case study 4

Community member: Is this really something you can teach? Don't kids either have good character or they don't?

CHAPTER 2

Character Education

Do you recognize the following?

Teacher 1: Are we allowed to teach values? Isn't it illegal?

Teacher 2: The whole problem with kids today is the parents' fault. If they did their job, we wouldn't have to teach this.

Teacher 3: I don't have time for another add-on. We are already expected to teach too many extras. I don't have time in the school day, and I don't want to do one more lesson preparation.

Parent: I don't want you teaching values to my child. We have our own values and we believe they should be taught at home.

Parent 2: This country is founded on Christian values, and that's what we should be teaching.

Community member: Back to the basics, that's what schools need. There's too much fluff, touchy-feely stuff, psychology, self-esteem and newfangled ideas in schools. What kids need to learn is what they used to teach in school: the Three Rs (reading, writing and arithmetic).

Moral Education

Character education is a form of moral education (Pritchard, 1988). Moral education is a broad umbrella covering student knowledge, understanding, intentions and desires, attitudes, and behavior in relation to what is right or wrong. The word "moral" is concerned with fundamental judgments and precepts about how people should behave and act, and the reasons for such behavior. Moral education is teaching about right and wrong.

Definition of Character Education

Character education differs from other forms of moral education in that it describes and prescribes what is meant by right and wrong (good and bad), and it is meant to help children behave in morally good ways.

Character education is intentional, conscious, planned, pro-active, organized, and reflective rather than being assumed, unconscious, reactive, subliminal, or random. One college professor said, "All education is character education." This is like saying, "Life is education." While both statements are true, there is a need for schools and professional educators who make conscious, informed decisions about curriculum, assignments, and classroom climate, how class time is spent and how students are assessed. If character education is so infused that neither the teacher nor the student knows it is taking place and if the teacher has not made conscious plans to teach for character, then it is not the kind of character education described in this book. However, once a teacher truly understands what character education is and implements the principles outlined in this book, all of education will be character education, because it is infused in a comprehensive way.

Universal Values

The first concern most people have is "Whose definition of good? Whose values system will be taught? Who is to say what is right and what is wrong? Who are you to tell me or my child what is right or wrong?"

The only values taught in character education are those all rational people agree are necessary. They are called **universal** (Lickona, 1991). Universal values are upheld by every civilized culture, religion, and belief system (Ryan, 1986). They are rational, objectively valid moral requirements to which all people are accountable. In fact, society cannot exist without them. A study of all major civilizations and religions gleaned the virtues that are held in common. This multicultural wisdom is called the Tao (Lewis, 1947). It shows that there is a common moral ground. There is a unifying morality, and children very much need to learn about it. In fact, educators have an obligation to teach this common core of values to children. Through character education, a common core of ethical values which transcend cultural, religious and socioeconomic differences is taught (Josephson, 1991; Whiting & Whiting, 1975). Certainly there are many differences in beliefs about right and wrong due to personal or private value systems. However, character educators believe it is a myth that all morals are individual, personal, and situational.

What exactly are the universal values? Surprisingly, there are many (Unell & Wyckoff, 1995). Separating universal and personal values is extremely important. Here are tests used to determine universal values:

Golden Rule Test. Is this a trait which I should display toward others and which I wish others to display towards me?

Everyone Test. Do we want everyone to have this trait? The question is not "Do we want everyone to display this trait all the time?" All character traits have to be demonstrated wisely. For example, when my son says to his sister, "You're ugly!...Mom, I was honest," this is not an appropriate display of honesty. There is a time when honesty is not the wise trait to display. We should be sensitive and tactful as well. Good judgment must be used to determine which virtue to use.

Opposite Test. Do we want children to act the opposite of the trait we are examining? If not, this may be a universal trait. For example, we do not want students to be dishonest.

Endurance Test. Is this trait an ideal that has been upheld throughout history in founding documents such as the Bill of Rights, speeches, literature, religious affirmation, art, music, and our cultural heritage?

Unity Test. Is there common agreement over this trait?

Public vs. Private Test. Is this trait needed to sustain public life and the common good, as opposed to private self interest?

Lists of Universal Values.

Because there are so many universal values, each community chooses the ones it wishes to emphasize. There are many lists from which to pick.

Plato wrote about four virtues: wisdom, justice, courage, and temperance. Franklin School, a charter school in Massachusetts, is based on these four pillars. Thomas Lickona (1991) states that there are two major values under which all other universal values fall. They are *respect* and *responsibility*. Respect means showing regard for the worth of others, self, property, animals, life, the environment, other belief systems, other cultures, and people of varying abilities or disabilities. Responsibility means acting upon convictions, being dependable, fulfilling our positive duties, and keeping our commitments.

The Aspen Declaration, an outgrowth of a character education summit in Aspen, Colorado, in 1991, chose six pillars: trustworthiness, respect, responsibility, fairness, caring, and citizenship.

Many state constitutions describe the purpose of education in terms of character education. The New Hampshire constitution states, "public schools should countenance and inculcate the principles of humanity and general benevolence, public and private charity, industry and economy, honesty and punctuality, sincerity, sobriety and all social affections and generous sentiments among the people." The Baltimore County School District adopted twenty-three values: compassion, courtesy, critical inquiry, due process, equality of opportunity, freedom of thought and action, honesty, human worth and dignity, integrity, justice, knowledge, loyalty, objectivity, order, patriotism, rational consent, reasoned argument, respect for others' rights, responsibility, responsible citizenship, rule of law, self-respect, and tolerance (1983).

A committee of the Association for Supervision and Curriculum

Development (ASCD) headed by Kevin Ryan in 1988 listed these universal characteristics of the morally mature person:
* respect for human dignity
* care for the welfare of others
* the integration of individual interests and social responsibility
* demonstration of integrity
* being able to reflect on moral choices
* seeking peaceful resolution of conflict

Some traits refer to the **treatment of people**, called *prosocial* behavior. Good character is needed for personal relationships such as marriage and family, as well as for civic duty. Attitudes toward people may include cooperation, helpfulness, compassion, friendship, respect for the bodies and feelings of others, respect for life, liberty and equality, participation in community life, tolerance, and helping the less fortunate. Martin (1989) called for mastery of the three "Cs": care, concern and connection, which are essential for carrying on society's economic, political, and societal processes. **Personal integrity** may include having a healthy life-style, having the courage of conviction, following one's conscience, and having positive self regard. Attitudes **toward work** may include pride in quality work, being reliable and punctual, showing a willingness to work, a sense of duty, good decision making, persistence, and being able to evaluate one's work. Attitudes **toward animals and the environment** may include animal rights and various forms of respect for nature.

The purpose of character education is to promote the personal and civic virtues needed for peaceful and harmonious community. Public and traditional values are reinstated as goals to reach toward.

Personal Values

How do people of character treat others whose value system is different from their own? With respect and tolerance. People do not have to agree on all values. They can agree to disagree and respect each other. Families and family value systems are treated with respect and dignity.

Values Clarification, an approach to moral education that was popular in the 1960s and '70s, treated all values as personal. No universals were recognized, and everyone's value system was considered unique. The impression given was that any value system is okay, that students have the freedom to decide what they want to believe, and that their wisdom in choosing is equal to that of adults. In contrast, character educators believe that there are clear rights and wrongs.

When students reach adolescence they become interested in differences of belief. They enjoy hearing and presenting two opposing sides to an issue. The teacher of adolescents should clearly state and uphold universal values and civic virtue. When the subject under discussion presents two "right" sides, the teacher objectively and dispassionately provides opposing viewpoints. If the teacher has strong personal views that are not shared by the families and cultures of the students, there are several ways to deal with it. For example, if the teacher feels strongly about the role of a particular religion, abortion, capital punishment, assisted suicide, or some other controversial issue, either each side is described equally well or people from both sides are brought in to present their viewpoints in light of universal values.

Teachers cannot use the school as a platform for promoting their personal value systems. They may have very strong personal opinions that are contrary to those of the students' families, but the school is not the place to promote personal value systems. Neither is it the place to ridicule, put down, or dismantle the value systems of the families of students. A teacher may have prejudices against certain religious or political groups, but the school is not the place to air them. Teachers are perceived as authorities by their students, and a teacher's personal opinion carries weight, so there is an ethical obligation not to use the teaching position to advance personal causes or beliefs that are contrary to those of the community. Teachers do have an ethical obligation to promote universal values.

Multiculturalism and Values

In the past decade there has been an emphasis on diversity: accepting and supporting a variety of cultural viewpoints. Some people thought diversity negated universal values. However, a common core of shared values is essential to appreciation of multiculturalism and diversity. The purpose of multiculturalism is to learn about the good in all cultures, and to appreciate their unique demonstrations of goodness. The reason we can admire other cultures is because they have found distinctive ways to promote the values in which we all believe. For example, here is a story from Bill Robb, a leading expert on character education in Scotland. He tells about a South African culture in which it is impolite to talk softly in public. Anyone who talks softly is seen as secretive, plotting no good, and rude; so they speak in very loud voices so that all can hear what they say. In our culture it would be impolite to speak loudly in a large group. We have the opposite customs, but the same shared value: courtesy and respect for others. Every culture, including South Africa's and our own, has injustices which we do not admire or want to emulate. If we study this aspect of a culture, it is for the purpose of keeping ourselves from making the same mistakes.

Angelo Giamatti, president of Yale University, has pointed out that diversity can be constructive: "Pluralism does not mean... the absence of standards... It signals the recognition that people of different ethnic groups and races... and personal beliefs have a right to coexist as equals under the law and have an obligation to forge the freedoms they enjoy into a coherent, civilized and vigilant whole" (Baltimore, 1983, p. 5).

Terminology: What Do We Mean?

Moral education in the context of this book refers to teaching the broad universal concepts of right and wrong, rather than a particular culture's standards.

Values education is a term often used synonymously with character education. It has been criticized because it implies values of relative worth that may have nothing to do with morality. For example, jewelry is valued and considered a valuable but its moral value is open to question! However, many character education programs are referred to as values education because they are restoring virtue to a valued place in the curriculum.

The term **traditional values** has been used to reflect those traits that have been considered valuable throughout history, but the term to some implies an opposition to progressivism. Character education in the context of this book combines the best of modern educational research with time-honored methods.

The term **virtues** suggests that there are cherished ideals. Aristotle used the term *virtue* as meaning moral or intellectual excellence or perfection as shown through habits. Unfortunately, the connotation of the word is old-fashioned or prudish and has been confused with virginity. When the term is used in this book, it refers to the cherished ideals of honesty, integrity, charity, prudence, etc.

Ethics, however, describes duties and obligations which are systematized. Classes in "ethics" tend to focus on unclear areas of moral decision making. It is important that teachers recognize that there are two aspects to ethics. First are the clear concepts of right and wrong, as outlined in a code of ethics. Students need to know what these are. On the other hand, there are ambiguous areas of moral life, places where there is not a clear right or wrong. Ethical reasoning helps deal with such dilemmas.

The term **character** can also be ambiguous. A child with a lot of personality is often called a "character." Students learn to analyze literature for its plot and characters. Character educators use "character" to mean the constellation of virtues possessed by a person. Others define character as knowing the good, loving the good, and doing the good.

Each of these terms is fraught with colloquialism as well. One person told me she objected to using the word "good" because of the connotation when she was growing up. So far there does not seem to be a term that is universally acceptable for describing this area, but by struggling with definitions we are increasing our skills in ethical literacy!

Why Character Education?

There are many reasons for including character education in schools:

* It is and has always been an important part of education.
* It is especially needed in today's society.
* It can't be avoided.
* It is the foundation for academic excellence.

Character Education Is Important

Throughout history it has been recognized that academic skills of themselves are not enough. When knowledge and skill are used for good, the benefit to society fully justifies them. But academic skills used for evil destroy society. For example, scientists using their skills to destroy life, mathematicians committing fraud and embezzlement, and musicians promoting rape and murder through their lyrics are misusing their skills in a way that harms society. One of the goals of Education 2000 is that the United States will be first in the world in math and science. However, Hitler had some of the greatest scientists in the world performing the most inhumane experiments on men, women, babies, and animals. Theodore Roosevelt said, "To educate a man in mind and not in morals, is to create a menace to society." A person who is skilled in other areas, but not morally, is a Frankenstein, a monstrous curse on society.

The message of character education is that there is an important moral mission to education. Core ethical values are the foundation of a democracy. The only way the United States will be able to maintain democratic freedom is if individual citizens have integrity and high moral character. It is possible to have human freedom only if individuals are moral. Freedom and morality are inextricably linked. The purpose of public schools is to help future citizens become both wise and virtuous.

Here is a letter that one principal sends to teachers at the beginning of each year:

Dear Teacher:
I am a survivor of a concentration camp. My eyes saw what no man should witness: Gas chambers built by *learned* engineers. Children poisoned by *educated* physicians. Infants killed by *trained* nurses. Women and babies shot and burned by *high school and college graduates*. So I am suspicious of education. My request is: Help your students become human. Your efforts must never produce learned monsters, skilled psychopaths, educated Eichmanns. Reading, writing and arithmetic are important only if they serve to make our children more humane (Ginott, 1972, p. 13).

Historical Support

The most important and fundamental task of every civilization has been that of communicating its moral standards and teaching children to follow them (Martens, 1981). Moral education has been a primary educational concern and integral in school curricula since ancient times (Ryan, in Vincent, 1996). Every great educator from Aristotle to John Dewey (1954) wrote about the need for moral education in schools.

Socrates, Plato, and Aristotle wrote that the purpose of education was to teach virtues such as mercy, tolerance, truth, justice, wisdom, courage, and temperance, and that the teacher was to be the conscience of the times. The Romans also extolled virtues such as courage, justice and self-control. Quintilian, Jerome, Comenius, and Herbart, all great educators, stated the importance of moral education. Rousseau and Kant believed that a school system should be based on universal moral laws such as the goodness and dignity of the individual. Kant (1899) wrote:

Man must develop his tendency toward the good. Providence has not placed goodness ready formed in him, but merely as a tendency and without the distinction of moral law. Man's duty is to improve himself; to cultivate his mind; and when he finds himself going astray, to bring the moral law to bear upon himself.

Man needs nurture and culture. Culture includes discipline and instruction. Genuine education should develop man's natural moral, intellectual and physical powers. Moral development begins in the home as the child responds to the mother's care and kindness.

Thomas Jefferson, Benjamin Franklin, and George Washington wrote extensively about the need for character education in American schools. Franklin and Jefferson, early American disciples of Kant, believed that democracy would fail unless the citizens were informed, highly self-disciplined and had a strong sense of right and wrong. Jefferson was an outspoken advocate of the need for teaching citizenship, patriotism, honesty, diligence, altruism, obedience, and self-discipline. Horace Mann (1891), the founder of public education in the United States, saw it as the agent for achieving social and political reform. He wrote:

> The common school is the greatest discovery ever made by man. . . Other social organizations are curative and remedial; this is a preventive and an antidote; they come to heal diseases and wounds, this to make the physical and moral frame invulnerable to them. Let the common school be expanded. . . and nine-tenths of the crimes in the penal code would become obsolete. . . property, life and character held by a stronger tenure; all rational hopes respecting the future brightened. Moral education is a primal necessity of social existence. The unrestrained passions of men are not only homicidal, but suicidal; and a community without a conscience would soon extinguish itself. . . But it will be said that this grand result [public schools] in practical morals is a consummation of blessedness.

John Dewey believed that education should be reformative in teaching proper moral conduct. In the early 1900s, Dewey developed a rational, scientific problem-solving method for teaching moral reasoning. He believed that education in the scientific process would do away with the evils of society.

Character formation was a component of every educational reform movement in this country (John, Collins, Dupuis, & Johansen, 1991). The Seven Cardinal Principles of Education, a reform movement in 1918, included "ethical character." The 1938 reform entitled Purposes of Education in American Democracy listed "civic responsibility." Goal 5 of the Education for All American Youth Reform in 1944 included "help to develop an appreciation of the ethical values which should undergird all life in a democratic society." The 1952 Education Policies Commission Goal of Education stated, "all youth need to develop respect for the other persons, to grow in their insight into ethical values and principles, and to be able to live and work cooperatively with others."

American education was built on a Judeo-Christian world view. The Jewish tradition placed a strong emphasis on moral education as part of an all-encompassing religious education. Early Christians also linked morality with religion. The Pietists brought a religious approach toward moral education to this country. Due to these religious roots, it was common practice in public schools to interweave moral messages with religious overtones into the curriculum.

In the 1960s and '70s, due to many social forces including court rulings regarding the removal of religious practices from the classroom, schools and teachers began to deliberately pull back from teaching morality. Most teachers would say, "We are not allowed to talk about that anymore. Right and wrong are a matter of individual belief. They are private matters." Teachers were expected to be neutral about moral issues, to teach that there were different opinions about right and wrong, and that there are no absolutes or universally upheld values. They stopped using the words "right and wrong," moving to terms like "appropriate and inappropriate." There was a deliberate, conscious stripping of morality from the curriculum of the school. Moral education was replaced with Values Clarification (Raths, Harmon, & Simon, 1977), an approach based on moral relativism. This approach encouraged students to question and even disdain traditional values and acquire their own personal value systems. Rather than challenge students to be honest, trustworthy, or responsible, the presiding virtue became believing in one's self and one's own value system. Self-esteem programs, pluralism, and secularism flourished.

Decline In Morality
Moral behavior in children began to radically decline as substance

abuse, vandalism, and violence increased. Problems in schools in the 1950s may have been not doing homework, throwing books, leaving lights on and windows open, throwing spitballs, and running in the halls. Now schools became concerned about weapons, drugs, murder, and sexually transmitted diseases. The average age of offenders kept getting younger, and there were at least 20,000 violent incidents per day in schools across the United States in the 1990s. These included rapes, burglaries, physical attacks on teachers, homicides, suicides, assaults and robberies, and abuse. Lives were at stake. Safety and health are issues schools can't ignore (Children's Defense Fund, 1996). The character education movement, which began to emerge in the 1980s, brought a revival of actively teaching virtues or universal values to children as an antidote to school and societal problems (Wynne, 1986).

The decline in morality was blamed on two sources: parents and the media. Changes in the family and society weakened the family's influence as a teaching entity. Parents began spending more time outside of the home working for economic survival and less uninter-rupted time with their children. Other societal changes that impacted families were: smaller, more isolated, more mobile and less stable families; stresses caused by open marital conflicts, family dysfunction, divorce, single parenting, and blended families; and the invasion of the home by television, telephone, radio, internet, computer games, and boom boxes. Television became the primary curriculum as children began watching it more hours than they went to school. Studies showed that it increased aggression. Even newspapers and news programs seemed to reinforce violence through headlines and extensive coverage. Movies, video games, toys, and music depicted violence, vulgar lan-guage, and the exploitation of women. Commercials, in a hypnotic and psychologically seductive manner, deliberately reinforced baser de-sires for sex, status, power, physical attractiveness, and materialism. Some people believed that because of these changes, educators had to shoulder more responsibility for moral education.

It would be a mistake to assume that all parents reneged on their responsibility as moral educators. There were conscientious parents who restricted media use and spent time teaching their children morals. They often found their efforts counter-cultural. Some felt that the school was tearing down the family values they worked so hard to instill. They saw Values Clarification used to criticize traditional values. Parents who experienced subtle and open hostility to their beliefs came to oppose any form of moral education in school.

Moral Issues Are Unavoidable

However, every day in the classroom teachers face moral and ethical issues that cannot be avoided. It is impossible to have a morally neutral school environment. When a student cheats on an exam, hurts another student, or defaces school property, the teacher cannot say, "I'm morally neutral."

There is a moral aspect to many parts of school life, beginning with whether to get up in the morning or stay in bed, whether to go to school or be truant, and whether to arrive on time or be tardy. Eating or not eating nutritious food affects school performance. Personal grooming, work habits, picking up litter, using time wisely and behavior on the playground have a moral component. Hundreds of moral decisions are made every day in the classroom.

Correlation of Character with Academic Excellence

Evidence is being gathered to show that children who have high moral principles do better in school and excel academically.

> We have enough evidence to say that when we help students develop the good side of themselves, we see academic improvement as well. Students become more cooperative and enthusiastic. The shift is especially dramatic among students who have been the most difficult for us to motivate. Bringing out the good in students may be one of the surest ways to raise test scores. It may be the only way to educate for lifelong learning (Harmin, 1990, p.1).

Summary

Character education is the most important goal of education. There is a historic mandate for teaching children to be both smart and good. Character education is needed as an antidote to societal problems exacerbated by the media and changing family structures. It complements the work of parents and families. Morality cannot be avoided. When character becomes a priority, academic excellence follows.

Exercises

Here are some exercises which have been used by many teachers introducing character education to their students.

1. *Have students draw a "good" person. This could be done as a small group, where one person lies on the paper and another traces around him or her. Around this person write adjectives or phrases which describe a good person. "A good person will be..."*

2. *"Please do, Please don't" exercise. Place students in groups of three to five. One person volunteers to be the Recorder. The Recorder takes a blank piece of paper and folds it in half, down the middle. The paper is opened and at the top of one column is written "Please do..." At the top of the other column is written "Please don't..." The group is encouraged to brainstorm appropriate behavior, or behavior which would be considered "good" and "right" for the "Please do" column, and behavior which would be considered "bad" or "wrong" for the "Please don't" column. These lists should include any behavior that is part of daily living, whether at school, home, or in the community.*

Answers to "Please do, Please don't" exercise from sixth graders in Merrimack, New Hampshire.

Please do...	Please don't...
have good manners	*fight*
be responsible	*smoke*
be honest	*steal*
tell the truth	*litter*
be honorable	*drink*
be courteous	*mouth back*
show respect	*lie, swear*

31

3. *Go back through your "Please do, Please don't" exercise or the "Good person" exercise and put a U next to the universal values. Put a P next to the personal values. If a trait is personal, could it be redefined as a universal? Using the tests, try to reach consensus over which values are universal.*

4. *Discuss: What is the most important thing to learn in school?*

5. *Make a list: What drives you crazy about kids today? Make a list of the problems you encounter. What character trait is missing?*

6. *Make a list of the moral decisions you have made today.*

7. *Discuss why academic excellence and good moral character often go hand in hand.*

8. *Role play the following situations and discuss your responses:*

   Case study 1

   Teacher: Are we allowed to teach values? Isn't it illegal?

   Case study 2

   Parent: I don't want you teaching values to my child. We have our own values and we believe they should be taught at home.

   Case study 3

   Parent: This country is founded on Christian values, and that's what we should be teaching.

   Case study 4

   Teacher: The whole problem with kids today is the parents' fault. If they did their job, we wouldn't have to teach this at school.

   Case study 5

   Community member: Back to the basics, that's what schools need. There's too much fluff, touchy-feely stuff, psychology, self-esteem, and newfangled stuff in schools. What kids need to learn is what they used to teach in school: the Three Rs (reading, writing, and arithmetic).

CHAPTER 3

Moral Leadership

Code of Ethics in the 1800s

Teachers each day will fill lamps, clean chimneys.

Each teacher will bring a bucket of water and a scuttle of coal for the day's session.

Make your pens carefully. You may whittle nibs to the individual taste of the pupils.

Men teachers may take one evening each week for courting purposes or two evenings a week if they go to church regularly.

After ten hours in school, the teachers may spend the remaining time reading the Bible or other good books.

Women teachers who marry or engage in unseemly conduct will be dismissed.

Every teacher should lay aside from each pay a goodly sum of his earnings for his benefit during his declining years so that he will not become a burden on society.

Any teacher who smokes, uses liquor in any form, frequents pool or public halls, or gets shaved in a barber shop will give good reason to *suspect his worth, intention, integrity, and honesty.*

The teacher who performs his labor faithfully and without fault for five years will be given an increase of twenty-five cents per week in his pay, providing the Board of Education approves.

Historically the teacher has always been viewed as a moral leader in the classroom. Students look to the teacher to give them moral direction and guidance. Leadership is often shown nonverbally, through body language such as posture, facial expressions, and movement. The teacher who conveys leadership (erect posture, pleasant facial expression, and a confident way of moving) has a positive effect on student behavior (Jones, 1987). Teachers, as leaders and models, must have, at a more advanced level, the virtues, knowledge and skills they expect of students. The foremost trait of teachers should be that they have high moral character, that they display the universal values we want students to acquire. Students learn from what teachers say and do. There must be a consistency of message and action for character education to be effective. Teachers must practice what they preach. The life of the teacher is in some ways an open book to students. The teacher's character sets the moral tone of the classroom.

Sermons We See

I'd rather see a sermon than hear one any day;
I'd rather one should walk with me than merely tell the way.
The eye is a better pupil and more willing than the ear;
Fine counsel is confusing, but example's always clear;
And the best of all the preachers are those who live their creeds
For to see good put in action is what everybody needs.

I can soon learn to do it if you'll let me see it done;
I can watch your hands in action, but your tongue too fast may
    run
And the lecture you deliver may be very wise and true,
But I'd rather get my lessons by observing what you do;
For I might misunderstand you and the high advice you give,
But there's no misunderstanding how you act and how you live.

One good person teaches many, we believe what we behold;
One deed of kindness noticed is worth forty that are told.
Who stands with those of honor learns to hold honor dear,
For right living speaks a language which to everyone is clear.
Though able speakers charm me with their eloquence, I say,
I'd rather see a sermon, than to hear one, any day.

Author Unknown

Teachers face many moral decisions every day. It is crucial that they have the highest ethical standards. This means showing respect for students and their families, as well as for colleagues and administrators. It includes resolving conflicts openly and honestly.

The Crab and His Mother

An old crab said to her son, "Why do you walk sideways like that, my son? You ought to walk straight." The young crab replied, "Show me how, dear Mother, and I'll follow your example." The old crab tried, but tried in vain, and then saw how foolish she had been to find fault with her child.

Aesop's Fables

Can a person of poor character teach character education? Can a person who does not know how to do math teach math? *Those who can, teach* is the name of a book by Kevin Ryan and James Cooper (1988). This concept refers to character education as well as other subjects.

I encourage teachers to write a code of ethics before school starts. This code describes the moral responsibilities they are committed to regarding students, families, colleagues, the administration, the community and the profession. The teacher presents the code of ethics as a commitment to the moral ideals of educators. A copy is displayed in the classroom and sent home to parents.

Here is a code of ethics written by Carmelle Lamothe, a teacher at Jewett Street School in Manchester, New Hampshire:

Regarding my students:

I am committed to...
- *Respecting each of you for your individuality.*
- *Doing my best to allow you some measure of success, regardless of your abilities.*
- *Being fair, truly listening to you, and being open-minded.*

- *Using every opportunity to let you know that I care deeply for you.*
- *Performing my duties as your teacher in a reliable and diligent fashion.*
- *Acting in a trustworthy manner, by being honest and keeping my promises to you.*
- *Always seeking to further your educational and moral development.*
- *Giving you opportunities to practice citizenship and global awareness.*
- *Developing a classroom environment in which you will experience the quality of life possible in an ethical community.*

This teacher continues her code of ethics with commitments to parents, the administration, her colleagues, and herself.

Here is an excerpt from the *World Monitor* magazine:

> Kids copy kids, but even more they copy adults. The adolescents ... deeply resent dicta from their elders that signal "do what I say, not as I do"... Show me parents and politicians who do not lie, or deliberately skid along the edges of untruth, and I will show you honest kids. Show me public media that do not demean women or minorities, and I will show you schools where discrimination and sarcastic stereotyping are readily addressed... One cannot reform the school if [teachers] by their actions signal contempt for the school's desired values... Then school reform starts with us? Indeed it does... It is about living the values which the school stands for... Silence about our responsibility is a costly oversight. Adult lives that mock the schools' proper values are living hypocrisy and breed cynicism in the young (Morality, 1992, p. 27).

Throughout history teachers have been expected to be models of good character. Here is a tongue-in-cheek description adapted from Jessie Stanton, written in 1920:

The Ideal Teacher

The teacher should have a strong physique and a strong well-balanced nervous system. She should be plump and round and have curly short hair. Her cheeks should be rosy and her teeth pearly white. She should have a pleasing personality and a quiet firm manner. She should be poised and of high moral character. She should have sentiment but not sentimentality. She should be gentle but not sloppy, strong but not impetuous when bitten or scratched.

She should have a fair education. By this I mean she should take a doctor's degree in psychology and medicine. Sociology as a background is advisable.

She should be an experienced carpenter, mason and plumber and a thoroughly trained musician and poet. At least five years' practical experience in each of these branches is essential.

She should be a close observer and a judge of character and should be able to deal with young and old. She should be able to hypnotize the parents of her young pupils and cause them to change lifelong habits of thinking in two parent meetings.

Here is her life story:

From early childhood she was given every sort of tool and taught to practice close observation. She spent every morning seeing and sawing. In the afternoons her time was spent on music, hearing, howling and handling. She spent her evenings practicing manners, masonry, mechanics, mesmerism and musing on metamorphosis. Thus she acquired early in life the inestimably useful habit of using every second to its highest capacity.

But, added to all these virtues and attainments, she should have a spine of steel to stand the long hours and the tremendous demands made upon her. Her spine must bend easily, however, so that she can crawl under radiators with the cleaners to dig out the pencils or put away books on shelves close to the floor. She should have feet of iron so that she can go up and down stairs tirelessly all day long from cafeteria to roof to classroom to office. Now she has studied, **now at 83 — she is ready to teach!** (Stanton, 1954).

While teachers have legal obligations as defined by court cases, legislation, and staff handbooks, our goal is that teachers maintain high ethical standards by displaying good character. Ethical behavior is more important than any other aspect of teaching. An ethical teacher needs to have an awareness of moral issues, a sense of right and wrong, good judgment, integrity, and courage.

Ethics vs Laws

Laws and ethics are not the same thing. Ethics are internalized commitments to right conduct and the ideals of the profession. They are monitored from within the individual, organization, or profession. It has been said that ethics are the invisible laws and concepts. Laws are codified public statements which are monitored by external powers. Laws are not always ethical, although we want laws based on ethical principles. Conversely, there is a great deal of unethical conduct that is legal. Most codes of ethics are voluntary: people choose to commit to them, whereas laws are requirements.

Laws	Ethics
externally monitored	internally monitored
requirements	recommendations
defined by government	defined by professionals
describe minimum standards	describe high standards and goals
are imposed	voluntary commitment
infractions are punished	describe beliefs and philosophy

Definition of Ethics

A code of ethics expresses moral principles and ideals. Ethics are systems or codes of morals, statements about right or good ways to conduct one's self. Ethics are especially important in preventing the abuse of power. The people in power have an obligation to protect the interests of the less powerful. Ethics are guidelines to prevent potential harm to the interests of the less powerful. The greater the gap in power, the more ethics are needed. Codes of ethics encourage people in power to use professional judgment in deciding what is best for the less powerful, as opposed to what might be easiest or popular. Ethics are established to cope with temptation and destructive impulses, to promote what is right over what is expedient, and to give support for acting upon what is right (Wynne & Ryan, 1993).

A codes of ethics may contain the following categories: 1) ethics toward students; 2) ethics toward families; 3) ethics toward staff members; 4) ethics toward administrators; 5) ethics toward the profession; 6) ethics by students toward others (NAEYC, 1974; Feeney & Kipnis, 1992).

Here are specific guidelines for ethical conduct in each area. They come from many different published ethical codes, as well as from personal experience. Statements are numbered so that they can be used as reference points when dealing with ethical problems.

Ethics Toward Students

1. Students are treated with respect and dignity regarding:
    a. race, ethnicity, national origin
    b. religion
    c. gender
    d. physical attractiveness
    e. socioeconomic status
    f. ability or disability
    g. health or diseases
2. The teacher recognizes and respects the uniqueness and potential of each student even when there are perceived deficiencies.
3. Students are given the very best care and education of which the teacher is capable. Students are protected and kept safe and free from danger through:
    a. care of the environment
    b. proper supervision
    c. adequate planning (foresight)
4. Students are not harmed physically or psychologically. Students are not deliberately humiliated, shamed, degraded, exploited, intimidated, or placed in danger.
5. Adults do not engage in any form of sexual relationship or other

sexual misconduct with students, including acts, language, and pictures.

6. Symptoms of child abuse and neglect are reported to the proper authorities.

7. The teacher establishes only those relationships which promote the social, emotional and academic growth of students. Teachers do not fraternize with or date their students.

8. The teacher does not advocate, use in front of at school functions, or provide controlled and illegal substances to students.

9. Problems with students are not talked about to others in front of them. Negative information is only shared with the people who need to know.

10. The teacher handles information about students honestly and tact fully.

11. The teacher does not use his/her position to influence students regarding politics and religion. Favoritism is not shown toward those whose political and/or religious positions are the same as those of the teacher. Grades are not lowered because students disagree with the teacher. There are objective standards for grading.

12. The teacher does not tutor for pay or otherwise provide services for money to his/her students. The teacher does not accept gifts that are used to influence the treatment of a student.

> *"I've come to a frightening conclusion that I am the decisive element in the classroom. It is my personal approach that creates the climate. It's my daily mood that makes the weather. As a teacher, I possess a tremendous power to make a child's life miserable or joyous. I can be a tool of torture or an instrument of inspiration. I can humiliate or humor, hurt or heal. In all situations, it is my response that decides whether a crisis will be escalated or de-escalated and a child humanized or de-humanized."* (Ginott, 1972, p. 13)

Ethical Responsibilities to Children

We all feel a moral obligation to promote the welfare of children, so that they have clothing, food, shelter, discipline, quality education, medical and dental care. We want to safeguard children from abuse, violence, discrimination, and unwholesome influences. We want to provide them with good adult examples, a moral community and opportunities to develop good character, conduct, and habits. (From the Bill of Rights for Children, 1991; Children's Bill of Rights).

Ethics toward Families

1. Parents: are informed about the curriculum;
   a. planned activities
   b. school policies
   c. accidents if their child is hurt.
2. Parents are informed if their child is exposed to a contagious disease (Laws specific to AIDS make it an exception).
3. Parents have access to all records kept on their child, according to the Buckley Amendment.
4. Parents have the right to make decisions regarding what is in the best interests of their child. Sometimes those decisions will be different from the recommendations of the teacher. Their wishes are respected and followed when they do not want their child to participate in some activities.
5. Parents have the right to confidentiality and privacy. The teacher refrains from disclosing confidential information about the family, unless it is a case of neglect or abuse. Parents are not talked about to other parents or members of the community and only with staff on a "need to know basis." (If others "need to know" the information, it is passed on; otherwise it is not.)
6. Parents are informed about the progress of their child.
7. Official information about a child is not passed along to other people unless parents are informed first.

> *People have a right to information which affects them.*

8. Families are not discriminated against due to race, national origin, socioeconomic status, religious beliefs, physical appearance, or parenting style.
9. Families are treated with respect. The dignity of the family, its culture, customs, beliefs and religion, are respected.
10. Parents are welcome to visit the classroom at any time provided they do not interrupt the teacher and activities.
11. When parents volunteer in the classroom, they are treated with respect and their efforts are supported.
12. Parent volunteers have an obligation to keep confidential anything they learn about individual students and their families. When parents, teachers, student teachers, and researchers have been working in a classroom, they are ethically bound not to discuss negative information about individual students with others outside the classroom. The confidentiality of students and families must be protected.
13. When parents question a teacher's judgment, they talk to the teacher first, rather than going to other parents or administrators. If the issue is not resolved, they contact the teacher's immediate supervisor.
14. The teacher presents the school in a positive light to parents.
    a. The teacher does not complain to parents about the administrator or school policies.
    b. The teacher defends the program when it is criticized by parents.
    c. The teacher takes concerns expressed by parents to the administrator.
15. Parents are treated with respect during telephone conversations and conferences, even when they are hostile.

Guidelines for Conflicts between Parents and Teachers
- Do not be defensive and contradict each other.
- Listen.
- Say "Thank you for talking with me about this. Your perspective is important."
- Use active listening to show you heard what was said: Rephrase or summarize the other person's concern. "What you seem to be saying is..."
- Share information which bears on the issue.
- If the other party persists with his or her opinion, do not make a decision at that time. Say "Can we work on or think about this and meet again?" Then get advice from your supervisor.

Ethics toward Other Staff Members

1. The teacher establishes a relationship of trust and respect by:

   a) not talking about others behind their backs;

   b) openly communicating concerns directly to the person involved. **Invalidating another person is an unethical means of advocating a point of view. Seeking power by blocking the voices of other people is unethical (Evans, undated).**

2. The teacher maintains a positive approach.

   > *Begin the day with friendliness,*
   > *Keep friendly all day long.*
   > *Keep in your soul a friendly thought,*
   > *In your heart a friendly song.*
   > *Have in your mind a word of cheer*
   > *For all who come your way,*
   > *And they will greet you, too, in turn*
   > *And wish you a happy day.*
   >   *Author Unknown*

3. The teacher does not talk with other staff members in a way that denigrates:

   a. students;

   b. parents;

   c. other staff members;

   d. administrators.

Ten Commandments of Human Relations

I. Speak to people. There is nothing as nice as a cheerful word of greeting.

II. Smile at people. It takes seventy two muscles to frown, only fourteen to smile.

III. Call people by name. The sweetest music to anyone's ears is the sound of his/her own name.

IV. Be friendly and helpful. If you would have friends, be a friend.

V. Be cordial. Speak and act as if everything you do is a genuine pleasure.

VI. Be genuinely interested in people. You can like almost everybody if you try.

VII. Be generous with praise, cautious with criticism.

VIII. Be considerate with the feelings of others. There are usually three sides to a controversy: yours, the other person's, and the right side.

IX. Be alert to give service. What counts most in life is what we do for others.

X. Add to this a good sense of humor, a big dose of patience and a dash of humility and you will be rewarded manyfold.

Author Unknown

---

4. Each member of the staff has an obligation to be clear to an other about conflicts, without speaking about it with others. When the teacher has a concern, he/she first goes to the person it involves.

If the problem cannot be resolved, they both go to the person at the next level of supervision. There should be a written appeals policy which articulates the process so that it is conducted in an orderly way. Too often teachers who have a problem go to their supervisor's supervisor or other teachers first.

5. Support personnel such as aides, assistants, and volunteers are treated with respect and are supported in their own professional development. The teacher works with support personnel in a way that helps them be successful, not making demands they are incapable of meeting, but encouraging them to use the skills they have.

a. Expectations are clear and there is a written job description for them.

b. There is regular, open, honest communication with them through staff meetings, conferences, and informal conversations.

c. If support staff are not fulfilling their obligations, this is explained clearly to them and put in writing.

If the staff person changes and meets the obligation, the indiscretion is "forgiven and forgotten." If termination is necessary, there is written documentation of the problem as well as the date of the conference in which it was discussed.

Ethics toward Administrators

1. Each person has a right to information that affects him or her.

2. Administrators are treated courteously and with respect both to their faces and behind their backs.

3. Where there is a problem over policy, the teacher takes a role of advocacy by clearly articulating the problem and researching possible solutions. The purpose of bringing up problems is to work toward solutions and agreement.

4. The teacher does not "let things go" in order to prevent making waves, but is compelled to confront:
   a. misconduct;
   b. poor policies;
   c. observed inappropriate practices.

5. "Empowerment is not entitlement" means that expressing an opinion is ethical, but demanding that all agree is not. The purpose of each individual's communication within a group is to work toward agreement, even if it is agreeing to disagree (Evans, undated).

6. When there is a disagreement over policy, a confidential meeting is held with the administrator and the problem is explained clearly and in a constructive manner. The teacher recognizes that this may not alleviate the problem, but continues to research and bring more information to the administrator in a noncritical and positive manner.

7. Administrators have an ethical obligation to listen and treat seriously the concerns of others.

8. Administrators should not put down or attempt to get rid of people who disagree with them.

My Attitude

I promise myself:

To be so strong that nothing can disturb my peace of mind.

To talk health, happiness, and prosperity to every person I meet.

To make all my friends feel that there is something good in them.

To look at the sunny side of everything and make my optimism come true.

To think only of the best, to work only for the best and expect only the best.

To be just as enthusiastic about the success of others as I am about my own.

To forget the mistakes of the past and press on to the greater achievements of the future.

To wear a cheerful countenance at all times.

To give so much time to the improvement of myself that I have no time to criticize others.

To be too large for worry, too noble for anger, too strong for fear, and too happy to permit the pressure of trouble.

My attitude....is my life.

Author Unknown

Ethics toward the Profession

1. Teachers are engaged in lifelong learning regarding best practices, laws, standards, and current research.

2. Teachers have an obligation to speak up when policies or practices are not in the best interests of students. Sometimes parents and administrators who do not have a background in education or whose background is in a different field of education have inappropriate ideas about how students should be taught. It is necessary to remember that any demands made are because people want what is best for children. Requests should be treated with respect. The teacher

provides information about the best methods of teaching specific ages and subjects.

3. It is the teacher's ethical responsibility not to teach in a way that is contrary to good practice, but to educate others in a tactful and positive way about appropriate education. Unfortunately, since parents and administrators pay the salaries, it is easier to set up a program that keeps them happy at the expense of the students. Educators have an ethical responsibility to advocate good educational practice.

4. The primary focus of all decisions should be "What is best for the students?"

Statement of Commitment

As an individual who works with children, I commit myself to furthering the values of education. To the best of my ability I will

- Respect and support families in their task of nurturing children.
- Respect colleagues and support them in maintaining ethical behavior.
- Serve as an advocate for children, their families, and their teachers in community and society.
- Maintain high standards of professional conduct.
- Recognize how personal values, opinions, and biases can affect professional judgment.
- Be open to new ideas and be willing to learn from the suggestions of others.
- Ensure that programs are based on current knowledge of development and education.
- Continue to learn, grow, and contribute as a professional.
- Honor the ideals and principles of good teaching.

(Adapted from the National Association for the Education of Young Children, 1974; Lanier & Cusick, 1985).

Ethical Issues Teachers Monitor in Students

While teaching ethics begins with personal example, it does not stop there. Students have to be taught ethical conduct, especially regarding school life (Ethics Resource Center, 1994). Three major issues to address with students are academic honesty, harassment, and discrimination.

Academic Honesty

One of the ethical problems of which students need to be aware is plagiarism. Plagiarism is using someone else's words, thoughts, ideas, or work without giving proper credit (full and clear acknowledgment) to the writer of the original. Whether plagiarism is intentional or unintentional, it is a serious and unethical offense (from Modern Language Association guidelines).

Academic dishonesty includes but is not limited to the following actions:

1. Submitting another person's work as one's own. This includes copying during examinations; purchasing term papers or reports; copying or purchasing laboratory reports, art work, homework, or computer work.

2. Providing or using unauthorized books, notes, or other sources of information during a quiz or examination.

3. Doing work for which another person will receive credit. This includes allowing one's reports, laboratory results, art work, homework, computer work, or examination answers to be submitted by another person as his or her work.

4. Falsifying or fabricating data results from research or field work.

5. Using unauthorized assistance on an assignment.

6. Falsifying, through forgery or other alteration, academic documents such as grade reports, progress reports, parent/teacher communications, doctor's excuses, transcripts, test scores, and official school records.

7. Stealing, mutilating or destroying school property such as library books, periodicals, school books, or computer information systems.

8. Stealing, copying, or destroying another person's computer program or file, deliberately preventing another's access to the computer system, or impeding the system's performance.
9. Stealing, mutilating, destroying, or falsifying the property of a teacher or other student. (Adapted from Notre Dame College Academic Honesty Policy, 1995).

Harassment

Everyone should be able to work and learn in an atmosphere of respect for the dignity and worth of all.

Sexual harassment is offensive behavior that includes unwelcome advances and requests for sexual favors, as well as physical conduct and expressive behavior of a sexual nature wherein:

- submission to such conduct is made either explicitly or inexplicitly a condition of an individual's academic or social standing and/or;
- submission to or rejection of such conduct by an individual is used as the basis for academic decisions affecting that individual, and/or;
- such conduct has the purpose or effect of unreasonably interfering with an individual's performance or creates an intimidating or offensive environment.

Conduct which may be considered sexual harassment in any relationship other than between two consenting peers includes such things as verbal harassment or abuse; subtle pressure for sexual activity; sexist remarks about an individual's clothing, body, or sexual activities; unnecessary touching, patting, or pinching; leering or ogling of an individual's body; constant brushing up against an individual's body; demands for sexual favors accompanied by implied or overt threats concerning one's grades or status; physical assault; and displaying sexually suggestive objects or pictures.

Harassment is any offensive behavior that includes unwelcome advances, bullying, name calling, or ridicule. Harassment may be based on a physical characteristic or sociological condition such as name, weight, height, skin color, intelligence, physical flaw, place of birth, or place of residence. Students are expected to treat the bodies and feelings of others with respect, to respect each other's space, and to refrain from physically or psychologically harming or intimidating others.

Discrimination

Federal law requires schools to oppose any form of discrimination, whether on the basis of race, color, national origin, sex, age, religion, handicap, disability, or sexual orientation. Discrimination or prejudice refers to having an unfavorable attitude of a hostile nature regarding a particular group, or demeaning behavior or language toward a class of people.

a. Racial slurs are unacceptable. Nicknames which refer to specific groups (nigger, spick, chink, etc.) are not allowed on school grounds or at any school function.

b. Students with handicapping conditions have the right to a free and public education. They are not to be excluded from participation or denied a benefit because of the handicap. They should have access to all the services provided for non-handicapped students.

c. According to the Modern Language Association and American Psychological Association (1995) guidelines for writing, students are expected to use inclusive language. "He," "him," and "his" are unacceptable pronouns when referring to females. The term "man" is not used when referring to females. Many masculine terms have been changed to better describe both genders. For example, *fireman* has become *fire fighter, mailman* has changed to *mail carrier*, *policeman* to *police officer*.

The Use of a Code of Ethics

Each individual educator should ascribe to a code of ethics. Some teachers and school districts write their own to reflect local issues and practices. Other professional organizations like the National Education Association, sports organizations, schools administrators' organizations, and special educators, have written codes of ethics.

How are these codes used? Their primary purpose is to develop an **awareness** of ethical issues and appropriate ethical conduct. This awareness should lead to **self assessment** and **planned improvement**. Because the code of ethics describes areas where educators often fail, there needs to be regular, rigorous, private self-assessment of one's decisions and behavior.

Sometimes a **commitment** to ethical conduct is pledged. Educators may make a public commitment, either in writing or orally.

The code of ethics may provide **benchmarks for evaluation**. For example, if an educator's supervisor performs a yearly evaluation, the code of ethics may be referred to.

Myself

I have to live with myself, and so
I want to be fit for myself to know:
I want to be able as days go by
Always to look myself straight in the eye:
I don't want to stand with the setting sun
And hate myself for things I've done.

I don't want to keep on a closet shelf
A lot of secrets about myself,
And fool myself as I come and go
Into thinking that nobody else will know
The kind of person I really am;
I don't want to dress myself up in sham.

I want to go out with my head erect,
I want to deserve all people's respect,
But here in the struggle for fame and pelf,
I want to be able to like myself.
I don't want to think as I come and go
That I'm bluster and bluff and empty show.

I never can hide myself from me,
I see what others may never see,
I know what others may never know,
I never can fool myself — and so,
Whatever happens, I want to be
Self-respecting and conscience free.

Edgar Guest

Some organizations have an **ethical review board** composed of peers in the profession. Colleagues or parents may bring an educator before the ethical review board. This board of peers will either dismiss a charge, absolve, apply censure or sanctions, demand corrective measures, or in severe cases, recommend revocation of the teaching credential. The ethical review board provides accountability, but is also perceived as punitive. There are ambiguities, nuances, and different interpretations of any code of ethics. Whose interpretation is correct? Can a code of ethics be misused in such a way that good teachers are punished? Teachers may disagree with elements of the code. Does this mean that they cannot teach? The idea of an ethical review board for educators is relatively new and has brought a feeling of wariness to many.

Summary

In an ethical environment, everyone treats others with respect and in a positive manner. It takes commitment and effort to work with other human beings (colleagues, parents, administrators, and students) in a positive way. A team approach is necessary. Time has to be spent talking together and sharing with each other in a supportive way. The various team members are respected for their diversity of viewpoint. Team members share comradeship but not at the expense of individual differences. Each person is encouraged to present a different point of view. Problems are handled confidentially and in an open, honest, productive manner. In an unethical environment people criticize each other, sometimes openly, but more often behind each other's backs. In an ethical environment the morale is good because people like each other and show it. In an unethical program people are unhappy and either show it blatantly or subtly. In an unethical environment people blame others (often the administrator or parents) for problems rather than looking for constructive ways to improve themselves.

While most educators agree that a code of ethics is important and that teachers need to be made aware of ethical issues, there is disagreement about how the code should be applied and how accountable teachers should be to it.

Exercises

These are exercises which both students and teachers have used to apply their understanding of ethics.

1. *Write a personal code of ethics and statement of commitment or ascribe to one such as that of the NEA or NAEYC. This code or statement of commitment should be shared with students, parents, colleagues, and administrators.*

2. *List the core values which teachers need to show. Give an example of how teachers show that core value. Then give a non-example (in which teachers are not showing that core value).*

Core Value	Example	Non-example

We asked a group of thirty teachers to describe the character traits or ideals of teachers. Here are some of the traits they listed. Notice how these are traits teachers want to see in students as well.

An ethical teacher is:

able to work well with colleagues
accountable
aware of individual differences
caring
committed
committed to excellence
compassionate
conscientious
consistent
cooperative
democratic
dependable, prompt
diligent
drugfree
encouraging/supportive
ethical
fair
forgiving
friendly
hard-working

helpful
honest, admits shortcomings
humane
humble
inclusive
kind, caring
knowledgeable about subject matter
literate
moral
patient
prompt
punctual
reliable
respectful of others
responsible
self-disciplined
unselfish
sincere
persistent
trustworthy

Another group of teachers organized character traits valued in teachers as follows:

Have a positive attitude; show enthusiasm; be cheerful and uplifting; have a sense of humor and positive self-image; be honest and trustworthy; show a willingness to be innovative, creative, resourceful, a learner, self-motivated, risk taker, compassionate, respectful, a team player, consistent, flexible, cooperative, a good communicator, approachable, reliable, punctual, physically, mentally, and emotionally well.

3) Using blank pieces of paper for each category, list ethical obligations and problems in each:

1. Toward students

2. Ethical behavior by students

3. Toward families

4. Toward staff members and administrators

5. Toward the profession

A group of teachers wrote these character traits for each section:

***Toward students**: fair, meet individual needs, stay current, meet curriculum requirements, criticize actions, not students, don't impose personal beliefs on them, don't abuse grading power, build self-esteem of students.*

***Ethical behavior by students**: respect each other and teacher, follow the Golden Rule, be cooperative, resolve conflict, work together, value ideas of others.*

***Toward families**: open lines of communication, don't blame the parents, don't compare children with siblings, don't judge based on stereotypes, right to privacy, right to be included in the education process, recognize their responsibility to care for and meet needs of their child, don't misinform.*

***Toward staff members**: team player, willing to accept criticism, diplomacy, helpful, supportive, share ideas, honesty: don't take other people's things, keep informed, respect other people's teaching phi-*

losophies, don't embarrass or confront them in front of students or other teachers.

Toward the profession: willingness to continually better self, learn new approaches, look like a professional, work for improvement, maintain high standards, obey laws, work for the improvement of the school, commitment to quality.

4) **Conflicts to role play** after reading the section entitled "Ethics toward Families": One person takes the role of the **parent**, another the **teacher**, and the third an **observer**. Rotate roles so each person plays the part of teacher.

Situation 1. Parent: Another kid is picking on my child. She's calling him names, pinching him, taking his lunch money.

Situation 2. Parent: We don't believe in Halloween. We think it's an evil holiday and we don't want anything about Halloween done in our child's class.

Situation 3. Parent: You gave our daughter a C and I think she should have gotten a higher grade. All her papers that she brought home were good, and I don't think that C is fair.

Situation 4. Parent: I think there's a personality conflict between you and my child. You and he just don't seem to get along. He says you don't like him and you are always picking on him.

Situation 5. Parent: I don't agree with the way you are teaching reading. I think kids need to learn phonics. I don't go along with all this new stuff about writing process. What they need is the good old drill in basic skills. I don't think these new methods are any good.

Situation 6. Parent: I think you give too much homework. My child gets home and has to study all evening. There's no time to play or do anything but homework.

Situation 7. Parent: My child says you disagree with my views on politics.

Situation 8. Parent: My daughter says that you are always picking on John, that you treat him unfairly.

Situation 9. *Parent: My child says you told him he would probably flunk if he took off for our religious holiday.*

Situation 10. *Parent: I want my child taught abstinence, and I don't want her to participate in your sex education program.*

Situation 11. *Parent: Let me know if my kid gives you any trouble, and I'll 'have his hide'.*

Situation 12. *Parent: Who's the kid whose always getting in trouble and disrupting the class? I don't think that's right. I'm going to talk to the principal about it. Why should my child lose out because you have to spend all your time with that other child?*

5) *Conflicts to discuss after reading the sections entitled: "Ethics toward Other Staff members" and "Ethics toward Administrators"*;

Ethical Problem 1. *Another teacher in the school tells you about a teacher who is "coming unglued," screaming at the students, choosing one favorite student, and being sarcastic to the others. All kinds of stories about this teacher are being told. What should you do and say? Why?*

Ethical Problem 2. *In the classroom next to yours a teacher is constantly putting students out in the hall. Some students are out there most of the day. There is always at least one child out there. What should you do? Why?*

Ethical Problem 3. *You are on playground duty and you find a group of boys watching two boys wrestle. When you go over to break it up, the kids say, "But Mr. Smith lets us do it." How should you respond?*

Ethical Problem 4. *You are walking down the hallway and you hear one white student taunt a black student by calling him "nigger" and saying, "Open your eyes and smile so we can see you in the dark." What should you do? Why? (The students are not in your class).*

Ethical Problem 5. *You are sent a memo from the director/principal stating a new policy with which you disagree. It asks all teachers to give more homework and to send home daily at least one worksheet which the students have completed. You don't agree with this. What should you do? Why?*

6) Case Studies to discuss *after reading the section, "Ethical Issues Teachers Monitor in Students"*

Case Study I: *Which version is plagiarism?*

Original Version

Transportation did not stop crime in England or even slow it down. The "criminal class" was not eliminated by transportation, and could not be, because transportation did not deal with the causes of crime.

Version A

Transportation did not stop crime in England or even slow it down. Criminals were not eliminated by transportation because transportation did not deal with the causes of crime.

Version B

Robert Hughes (1991) points out that transportation did not stop crime in England or even slow it down. The criminal class was not eliminated by transportation, and could not be, because transportation did not deal with the causes of crime (168).

Version C

Hughes (1991) argues that transporting criminals from England to Australia "did not stop crime.... The 'criminal class' was not eliminated by transportation, and could not be, because transportation did not deal with the causes of crime" (168). (from MLA)

Case Study II. *John was given an assignment to do a science project. Because he did not know how to use the tools, his father helped him. The poster said, "by John Smith." Was this academic honesty? Why or why not?*

Case Study III. *Students are given worksheets in social studies. During study hall they sit together to fill out the worksheet. Each student looks up a different answer and then shares it with the others in the group. They each turn in their own papers. Is this plagiarism? Why or why not?*

Case Study IV. *Mary says to Jane, "Do you want to meet in the library and do our homework together? I'll help you with your math* *if you help me with my English." They meet and work together, each turning in her own paper. Is this plagiarism? Why or why not?*

Case Study V. *Randy is weak in writing skills. After finishing his English paper, he uses spell check and grammar check on the word processor. He also asks his mother to read the paper and check it for errors. Is this plagiarism? Why or why not?*

Case Study VI. *Joe left his computer disk in the lab. Susan finds it and copies his lab report. The teacher reads the two lab reports and sees that they are exactly alike. Who has plagiarized? What should the teacher do?*

Case Study VII. *Marty says to Jennifer, "Hey, babe, what's up?" Is this sexual harassment? Why or why not? How should it be handled?*

Case Study VIII. *"Hey, crip, how you doin?" Fred says to his friend in the wheel chair. "Not bad. Yourself, nigger?" replies his friend. Is this discrimination? Why or why not? What should be done about it?*

Case Study IX. *The teacher hands out a quiz and is called to the office. Students begin opening their textbooks to look up answers. Is this plagiarizing? Why or why not? How should it be dealt with?*

Case Study X. *A student turns in a paper which is word-for-word the same as another student's. What should the teacher do?*

CHAPTER 4

Moral Climate

ETHOS AND ENVIRONMENT

Have you ever asked this question or heard these comments?

- *Teacher: Can my classroom really make a difference? The students are only with me for a short time. I can't change character, can I?*
- *Parent: I don't like what my kids are picking up at school. Trash language, bullying on the bus, mouthing off. I don't know what's going on, and I'm not sure they want me to find out, but I feel like giving those teachers a piece of my mind.*
- *Community member: Schools are a miserable failure. Kids come out acting worse and worse.*

The second way to implement character education is through the classroom climate. Climate pervades every corner of classroom space, every minute of the day, and every interaction that occurs in the room. Just as temperature, humidity, and wind cause geographical climate, the "weather"or environment of the classroom affects everyone as soon as the door is opened. It precedes curriculum and discipline.

A good environment is like an incubator, providing the atmospheric conditions or climate needed to develop character. It is like a womb, creating the best possible place for character development. This chapter examines ways that the teacher can make the classroom into a place where good character flourishes.

Safe Environment

The classroom is a safe haven for children in a violent world. Students should feel safe, both physically and psychologically. The environment should be checked daily to make sure it is physically safe: equipment is in good repair, furniture is sturdy, traffic paths are clear. There should be an emergency plan for fire, natural disasters, crisis, and violence. The teacher shows foresight in creating and maintaining a safe environment and being prepared for dealing with hazardous conditions.

Interactions among students are carefully monitored so that children are kept safe emotionally. The teacher deals quickly and decisively with peer cruelty, bullying, meanness, harassment, and any other behaviors that threaten students' feelings of safety. The behavior is stopped immediately. Discussion, dialogue, apologies, mediation, and other social consequences are some of the techniques teachers use (see the next two chapters). There needs to be a clear message that all students will be kept safe and protected, and will keep each other safe as much as possible.

Room Decor

For two years I taught in a private school and lived in an apartment beside the classrooms. I was surprised to find out how many people go through a school building after school, on weekends, and during vacations. As I gave tours of empty classrooms, it became clear to me that the room itself is an indicator of the classroom climate. The room gives a message to students, parents, and administrators. The room is a message. It shows priorities, goals, and philosophy. It reflects the personality and teaching style of the teacher in the same way that clothing styles and home decorations portray us. In fact, I have found, after visiting hundreds of classrooms, that a scrutiny of the classroom and daily plan, coupled with ten minutes for observing teacher/student interaction can provide enough information to predict the classroom climate.

Even though it has been said that good teaching can take place anywhere, the teacher finds ways to arrange the environment so that students receive messages from it. Signs, banners, posters, mottos, mobiles, and bulletin boards are print-rich ways to project moral messages.

Room decor begins with the entrance. Is it well marked so everyone can find it, even when the door is closed? Is it welcoming? One classroom at Northwest School in Manchester, New Hampshire, has this hand made poster on the door:

W hen you
E nter this
L ovely room
C onsider yourself
O ne of the terrific
M agnificent members who
E njoy exploring and learning

Descriptions of a good environment *(rate your room on each)*:

___ safe
___ purposeful and efficient
___ organized
___ clean and neat
___ uncluttered, spacious, and uncrowded
___ attractive and aesthetically beautiful
___ colorful
___ cheerful and friendly
___ inviting and accessible
___ motivating

Most of the room should be decorated with things made by the students. A sixth grade teacher had the students make posters about character traits and reported a change in atmosphere as they worked. He found that focusing on the character trait through an art project improved the classroom climate!

Display their artwork and writing samples concerning character in an aesthetically pleasing manner, mounted on colored paper and tacked up by all four corners. This gives students a sense of accomplishment and builds their self-esteem. Most of the decorations should be at their eye level, so the teacher needs to get down to the height of the children and look at the room from their point of view.

Use bulletin boards to promote character education. They should have a colored background and border, be easy to read, and be creative and colorful, with a clear focal point. A bulletin board should not be cluttered. Avoid putting up letters in yellow because they do not show up across the room. Teachers have used bulletin boards for character education in many different ways. One teacher encourages students to bring in newspaper clippings regarding moral issues. Another teacher has a bare tree at the beginning of the year. Each month there are different shaped "leaves" sitting at her desk. Whenever students see someone committing a "conscious act of kindness," they write the name of the person and what that person did on a leaf, then pin it to the tree. At the end of the month the tree is covered with leaves. Another teacher chooses a different character trait each month and puts up a display about that trait. There are word puzzles, stories, and other interactive activities on the bulletin board. Many teachers have a "student of the month," who decorates the bulletin board with family pictures and personal mementos. There may be a parent bulletin board near the entrance, with information for parents about the class, community events or classroom happenings.

Bulletin Board Checklist

____background	____border
____focal point	____attractive
____easy to read	____not cluttered
____colorful	____creative

Inspirational slogans and mottos can be used very effectively. Sheila Nudd, a middle school teacher at Hampton Academy in New Hampshire has a committee of students who choose a motto for each week. They get together periodically to go through books and choose the motto of the week. That motto is posted for all to see, is read at the beginning of the week as a starting point for reflection, and may be used for handwriting, journals, creative writing, discussion, or role play. One teacher has a graffiti board on which students can make up their own mottos (which must be signed).

Books in which appropriate mottos can be found:

Brownlow, P. (Ed.). (1993). *Dear teacher.* Fort Worth, TX: Brownlow Publishing Company, Inc.

God's little instruction book. (1993) Honor Books, Inc. PO Box 55388, Tulsa, OK 74155.

Phillips, B. (1993). *Book of great thoughts and funny sayings.* Wheaton, IL: Tyndale House Publishers, Inc.

Teacher's inspirations. (1990). Great Quotations, Inc. 1967 Quincy Court, Glendale Hts, IL 60139.

Wall, K. and Wall, L. (1992). *The road to success.* Walrus Productions, 4805 NE 106th St., Seattle, WA 98125.

Class goals and rules should be posted for all to see. There may be a class timeline showing each week or month of the school year and important events. Art prints may be borrowed from the local library. Portraits of heroes and heroines may be hung. Photographs of the students may be taken by the teacher, a designated class photographer, or brought in from home for display. Photographs are of high interest; they build self-esteem and a feeling that people care! Put a piece of clear plastic over the pictures so the students can point without ruining them.

The room should be decorated but not overdecorated. Create ambiance, an aesthetically pleasing atmosphere, and develop a sense of beauty and values through room decor.

Teachers spend a lot of time analyzing and rearranging the furniture because the floor plan contributes to the climate and exerts a strong influence on behavior. High quality space correlates with good teaching. There is no one way to set up desks. In fact they may be rearranged for different types of activities. Traffic paths are planned so students can move from one area to another without bothering others or tripping. The teacher can easily see and reach every area of the room. Each area has a clear and obvious purpose.

Here is a guide for creating a floor plan that enhances classroom climate.

1. Look at the overall room. Make a floor plan either on a piece of paper, flannel board, magnetic or chalk board. Draw the doors and other permanent features such as windows, sink, pencil sharpener, closets, and outlets.

2. Determine the main events of the day such as large group or meeting time, independent work, snack and meals (where appropriate), and small group work.

3. Block out the large group area first. There needs to be a place where the whole class meets. This may be the place for morning meeting, a class meeting, circle time, or whole-class presentation. It is important for building a sense of community. Students should not be facing the door or strong light such as a window. They need to have enough room to move. If a chalk board, overhead, or bulletin board will be used, students need to sit facing them. This area needs to have few distracting materials to touch or play with. Sometimes students sit in a circle on a carpet. Carpet squares or Xs made with electrical tape show where to sit. Sometimes a "magic carpet" is laid down and everyone sits around the edge of it. Bean bag chairs, floor cushions, and "whistle" chairs are used for informal meetings. Some

teachers prefer to have children sitting in chairs or at a table, especially when large group time involves doing paperwork.

4. The arrival and departure area is an important conveyor of climate. If your part of the country gets snow, there needs to be a place to put on and take off snowsuits and boots. Some classrooms have a mud room for this or a hallway outside the classroom.

There should be a place for each person to put personal items because a sense of belonging comes from having personal space. This space may be a tote tray, cubby, locker, desk, alcove, or file folder. Students need a place to put their backpacks, lunchboxes, hats, mittens, sweaters, extra clothes, boots, art projects, and beautiful creations. Where do students put assignments and projects they have completed and value?

5. High traffic areas need to be considered. They are usually the sink, wastebasket, drinking fountain, bathroom, and pencil sharpener. Traffic should flow easily around these areas so that students can move in an efficient and respectful manner.

6. There should be a small group area for teacher-led instruction of five to seven students. It should be away from noise and distractions, but the teacher needs to be able to see the rest of the room. In this area students have opportunities to interact with the teacher and each other in a way that fosters relationships.

7. Most classrooms have learning areas: small, clearly defined areas which contain materials, games, books, equipment, and activities for the students to use independently. In these learning areas students get their own materials and put them back afterwards, showing responsibility. The materials are easy to use and it is obvious how to use them. Most of the materials are open ended, there for exploration, investigation, or experimentation. When there is a "right answer," students can check their own work. These areas foster individual responsibility and peer interaction. Students working together practice cooperation, getting along with others, sharing, and solving problems. They serve as both leaders and followers. In these

areas students are usually interacting with each other, without direct teacher supervision. They may be discussing, working together, tutoring, studying as a group, or working on a group project. They are learning pro-social skills and the citizenship skills needed in a democracy.

Some areas may be study carrels where individual students work alone silently, increasing their sense of personal responsibility.

Sometimes tape on the floor is used to define an area. Other areas are defined by a carpet or table. Often furniture is used to block off certain areas. Dividers should be low, so that the teacher can see over them.

Examples of small group areas are: computer areas, book and magazine areas, a research area with reference books, educational game areas, art centers, writing or publishing tables, science areas, math centers, spelling tables, a drama stage, a listening center, and a special interest center for sports or another high interest topic.

8. Organize and label cabinets, shelves, and drawers. Orderly storage gives a message of organization. Books, reference and research materials, and computer disks are clearly labeled so that students can help in keeping the room neat. Tissues and cleaning materials should be kept in designated spots. Neatness is a character trait that is taught.

Use cabinet tops for plants, terrariums, aquariums, experiments, projects, models, kits, a globe, and reference materials. There should be space for records, those on individual students and the whole class (see chapter 9 on assessment).

9. The teacher is a visual decoration. Color of clothes, jewelry, tie, posture, eye contact, facial expression, and smell create climate. The teacher models habits of good health and grooming.

10. The room temperature, ventilation, and lighting also create climate. Natural lighting, open windows for fresh air, cleanliness, and good health habits contribute to a healthy climate, and they demonstrate the character trait of a healthy life-style.

Sound

Climate is created by sound as well as sight. The sounds in a room should be pleasant most of the time. Voice sounds should be pleasant (no yelling, screaming, or sarcasm) as the teacher talks with individuals and the whole class. Student names are used often (and not for misbehavior). Unfortunately, in many classrooms it is easy to figure out from the teacher's voice which students he or she does not like. It is worth taking the time to make an audio tape of thirty minutes of one's teaching in order to analyze negative voice tones. This does not mean the teacher needs to sound "sticky sweet" all the time. There is a place for firmness, disappointment, and even anger, but love has to come through as well. When students say, "The teacher doesn't like me," they are probably referring to voice tone.

Student-to-student interactions are highly imitative of teacher-to-student interactions. The teacher does not ignore negative voice tones among students. Students are expected to treat each other with respect and friendliness, and they are shown how to use voice tone to do so.

Sometimes the room is too noisy, causing frustration and confusion. Noise can be cut down by carpeting, curtains, ceiling tiles, and stuffed furniture. Teachers recognize that there is good noise and bad noise. Good noise indicates that everyone is on task and engaged in learning. Bad noise is caused by off-task, out-of-control behavior. The teacher and students control the noise. There should be time for silence. Maria Montessori believed that children learn best in a quiet atmosphere. She had the "Silent Game" in which students practiced being quiet. The teacher timed them and encouraged them to beat their own records. Silence can be a sign of peace and tranquillity.

Some teachers use music such as background music as students arrive and other types of music as students work. One teacher in Salem, New Hampshire, uses the small #78 r.p.m. records and 1950s music. When she gives a short assignment, she turns on the record player and tells students they have the length of the record to complete the assignment. It brings a chuckle to hear them singing along with golden oldies while working on their tasks. Other teachers use songs, often their own, to bring students together or get their attention during transitions. As students learn the songs, they join in.

There are several companies that produce songs about good character:

Laugh and Learn Life-skills. Regency Music, P.O. Box 141000, Nashville, TN 37217. This company has stories about honesty, obeying and kindness.

[Recorded by Vitamin L]. *Lovable Creature Music*, 105 King St., Ithaca, NY 14850, (607) 273-4175.

[Recorded by S. and C. Paton]. On *I've got a song, When the Spirit says sing.*, Folk-Legacy Records, Sharon, CT 06069.

[Recorded by Red Grammar]] *Teaching Peace.* Children's Group, Inc., 561 Bloor St. W., #300, Toronto, Ontario M551Y6 Canada.

Getting Along: The Children's Television Resource and Education Center, 330 Townsend St., San Francisco, CA 94107, (415) 243-9943.

Your Character Counts! Character Counts Coalition, (310)306-1868.

Character through the Classics. Learning Legacy, Capehart Ministries, 12507 Quincy Lane, Dallas, TX 75230, (214) 239-3850.

Interaction between Teacher and Student

Relationship-building between teacher and student is important to character education. Character is fostered through caring, concern, and connectedness (Brabeck, 1989). There is a parallel between relationship-building in the family and that of the classroom.

Before School Starts

In the family, it begins before birth. Mothers pat their stomachs and prepare for the baby throughout pregnancy. Relationships between students and teacher should also begin before school starts. The teacher may send a letter and picture to the students' homes. Teachers may make home visits or telephone calls. There may be an open house or orientation, a "Step Up Day" or social event where students and teachers meet each other. One school holds a family picnic on the first day of school so the teachers and families can meet each other. Some teachers begin the year by inviting students in small groups so as to have more personal contact. One teacher invites students to her home in groups of four.

First Day

The next phase of relationship-building in the family is face-to-face meeting at birth. Mothers commonly gaze into their newborns' eyes, and smile, and stroke their skin. Students too need eye contact, smiles, and physical contact from their teachers on the first day of school and when entering the classroom. Dr. Hal Urban, author of *Life's greatest lessons* (1997), stands at the door of his high school classroom and greets each student by name with eye contact, a smile, and often a handshake. I was sitting in the St. Louis airport after a national character education conference and shared this information about him with an assistant principal from Oregon. She said, "In all my years of administration I've only had one teacher who did that, and she never had a referral for a discipline problem." Positive interaction creates climate.

The components of positive interaction are:
- eye contact
- a smile, nod, or other positive facial expression
- use of the student's name correctly, often, and in a positive way
- physical touch through a handshake or other culturally appropriate manner which is acceptable to the individual student
- pleasant voice tone
- positive language: Rather than "do not" or "stop," state the positive expectation.
- an ability to dialogue: listen attentively as well as talk

- personal, individual attention (in large classes this may be through journalling back and forth to each other)
- courtesy
- beginning and ending the time together in a positive way with a greeting and goodbye.

Some teacher educators and school policies state that teachers should no longer have physical contact with their students because they might be accused of abuse. Of course school policy must be followed, but everyone needs appropriate physical contact. Students can learn the difference between good and bad hugs. Good hugs can prevent bad hugs. There are students whose only form of physical attention from an adult has come from sexual abuse. They need to experience appropriate physical affection. Here is an excerpt on hugging:

> *Hugging is healthy: It helps the body's immunity system, it keeps you healthier, it cures depression, it reduces stress, it induces sleep, it's invigorating, it's rejuvenating, it has no unpleasant side effects, and hugging is nothing less than a miracle drug. Hugging is all natural: it is organic, naturally sweet, no pesticides, no preservatives, no artificial ingredients and 100% wholesome. Hugging is practically perfect: there are no movable parts, no batteries to wear out, no periodic check-ups, low energy consumption, high energy yield, inflation-proof, non-fattening, no monthly payments, no insurance requirements, theft proof, non-taxable, non-polluting and of course, fully returnable.*

> *Author Unknown*

Respect is shown for the child's body. The teacher might ask, "May I give you a hug?" If the student's body language shows that he or she does not want to be touched, that right is respected. And of course a hug is given in a public place where others are present.

Quality Time

Every student needs quality time with the teacher. It takes skill to find time for individual students. I find myself using journal writing for this. In my college classes I pass out 4 in. x 8 in. index cards at the beginning of class. For the first five minutes, students take a one or two question quiz on the subject matter, writing their answers on the front of the card. The last five minutes of the class period are spent in writing their comments, thoughts and opinions, evaluation of the class, and questions on the other side of the card. I read these cards, write comments, and give them back at the next class. A bond develops through our written conversation. Students share more personally, and I have been given many helpful suggestions.

Some teachers are able to give undivided attention right in the middle of a large group exercise when everyone is busily involved in an assigned activity. Other teachers set aside their lunch time for eating with an individual student.

My first year of teaching, I taught sixth grade in southern Georgia. One girl was constantly disrupting the class, so I asked her to stay after school. We spent time visiting and getting to know each other. I never had trouble with her again, and she started influencing others to behave well!

Rudolph Dreikurs (1968) wrote about the four ingredients of positive relationships:

1) Mutual rights and respect. This must be demonstrated by the adult first.
2) Time for fun: spending time on what everyone enjoys.
3) Encouragement: A minimizing of mistakes, recognizing assets and strengths.
4) Communication of love.

The Campaign

Some teachers have proactively organized a campaign for the purpose of motivating students to want to have good character.

The two best sources for "campaigning" are political scientists running for elected office and, in the business world, marketing experts. They both have scientifically studied human motivation, how to get people excited about a candidate or a product.

Political campaigns include (but are not limited to): campaign buttons, bumper stickers, hats, t-shirts, balloons, signs, brochures, commercials, rallies, speeches, informal discussions, telephone calls, photographs, slogans, debates, and media attention. Lamar Alexander effectively used the plaid shirt to symbolize his campaign and walk across the state of New Hampshire before the primaries in 1996. Alan Keyes used a symbol of two golden keys.

Marketing experts have used commercials, billboards, brightly colored catalogues, mascots, and advertising brochures with pictures, logos, prizes, color codes, and other gimmicks to get people motivated to buy their products. Pencils, placemats, action figures, and pens are often given away. McDonald's is probably the world's best marketing expert to children.

There are teachers who have taken the same types of approaches in promoting good character. For example, students design a logo and then put it on t-shirts, hats, buttons, posters, and signs. They are creating a visual image of character education. Sometimes the colors chosen are symbolic of certain virtues. There may be a class flag or motto. A refrain, song, anthem, poem, spoken pledge, or cheer is used to rally students and get them excited about having good character.

Aristotle thought children should passionately fall in love with goodness (Aristotle, in Loomis, 1943). Unfortunately, most passions in our society are toward vice, rock bands, movie stars, brand name clothes, and professional sports. It is possible for teachers to elicit the same enthusiasm for goodness.

Summary

Classroom climate is foundational to character education. Climate is the general feeling created by an environment. A climate that encourages character development includes sight (room decor), sound (music and voice tones), and positive interactions. Teachers can promote a classroom climate fostering character education through a campaign.

Exercises

1. *Analyze your classroom for the messages it gives. Make plans for giving visual messages about character.*

2. *Make an audio tape of yourself teaching for thirty minutes. Analyze the climate conveyed through sound.*

3. *Give a survey to students. Ask them, "How does your teacher feel about you?" Have a smiley and frown face. Students mark the appropriate face.*

4. *Study a political or advertising campaign and choose the positive tactics you think would work in your classroom for promoting character education.*

CHAPTER 5

Moral Community

CLASSROOM MANAGEMENT AND GOVERNANCE

If "it takes an entire village to raise a child," what does it take to raise a village? The teacher is creating a "village" or moral community in the classroom. A moral community supports the character development of individual students.

How is a classroom turned into a community? How are twenty or thirty different individuals brought together as a working unit like that of a family? As students get to know each other, value each other, and work and play together, a moral community is formed.

This chapter describes a series of methods teachers use to craft a moral community. It begins with direct moral instruction from the teacher. The teacher reaches out and builds relationships with each student. The teacher/student bond creates a conduit for moral dialogue.

The teacher sets up activities through which students get to know each other, build friendships, and have a sense of community (Schulman, 1995). Moral exercises like class meetings, cooperative learning, role play, case studies, and debate are used to foster community building.

As students learn how to take responsibility for their own actions and learning, they also begin to take responsibility for the classroom and demonstrate civic virtue through various forms of democratic classroom government.

This chapter concludes by showing how to put these strategies into place at the beginning of the school year.

Direct Moral Instruction

As moral leaders, teachers begin by giving clear moral messages. Direct instruction was overused in the past and should not be the only method, but there is real merit in directly teaching virtues: what they are, why they are valued, and how they are demonstrated. After World War II, the free world was horrified by the indoctrination used in the Nazi educational system, and indoctrination became a bad word. But there is a place for the inculcation of goodness. It is appropriate to overtly teach about right and wrong and to use exhortation to instill a desire for goodness in students. Concepts such as repentance ("I'm sorry"), forgiveness, restitution, and apologies can be explained.

I use rides in the car for giving direct instruction to my children. My "captured audience" hears about my beliefs and values as I taxi them to school and around town. Teachers may begin each day with a short presentation on a virtue, what it means, why it is important, and how it can be demonstrated. In some classrooms a motto, proverb, or famous quotation is read and written on the board at the beginning of each day. Other teachers use pledges or verses for group recitation.

Sometimes direct instruction is in the form of a story. Fables and parables are short stories with a stated moral. *Chicken soup for the soul, The book of virtues, The moral compass,* and *Call to character* (see References) are books with short, readable stories and poems. Another old-fashioned way of teaching morals is the object lesson. A teacher might show a weaving and explain that some parts of our lives are already selected for us, like the warp, but we make our own decisions, like the woof. The weaving may have a mistake, and our lives also may have places where we made bad choices. Bringing an object for students to look at helps to focus their attention, and they remember the lesson better.

I try to begin each of my classes with a reflection. I put up a motto to look at and then read a short poem, passage, or anecdote that gives a moral message tied to the topic of the day.

Policies and Procedures

Educators teach behavior. Procedures are specific, clearly stated, positive behaviors which demonstrate good character (Canter & Canter, 1992). Every organization has policies and procedures in order to run efficiently. The same is true of the classroom. Procedures which are consistently followed help students develop habits of good conduct. Procedures are demonstrations of universal values. Students need clear expectations and high standards. These are often outlined through a standard of conduct or policy manual. The teacher needs to help students make connections between rules of conduct and virtue. When students learn to listen, they are practicing courtesy and respect for others. When they are economical with resources such as paper, books, rulers, calculators, pencils, maps, and desks, they show prudence and respect for property.

There is a procedure for each time of the day, as well as commonly occurring situations. More procedures may be added throughout the year as needs arise.

Procedures cover the following kinds of things:

Arrival time. What do students do when they arrive in the class-room?

Large group time. Students have to be taught to sit and listen, to stay in one spot, keep their hands to themselves, look at the teacher, and be quiet as a way of showing respect and courtesy.

Clean-up time. Students are responsible to keep the room clean, as well as their own areas.

At Jesse Remington High School in Candia, New Hampshire, each student has an assigned cleaning chore at the end of the day. It takes three to five minutes to complete the chore and replaces some of the janitorial service.

Outdoor time. There need to be procedures for going outside and for behavior on the playground.

Departure. Students need to know how to end the day in an efficient way.

Lining up. There will be times when students need to stand in line. Clear expectations need to be given regarding space between students.

Manners with visitors. People may visit the classroom. Students need to be told what to say and do when there are visitors. What should they do when a lesson has been interrupted and the teacher has to talk with the person at the door?

Toileting. There should be a system for leaving the room. Students need to be taught or reminded how to use the toilet, wipe up spills, flush after use, and wash hands.

Getting a drink. There needs to be a procedure so students can get drinks without interrupting the teacher and the class. The water bottles now available make this task easier.

Obtaining help from the teacher. Students will want to talk with the teacher at times when the teacher is busy with other students. A signaling system can be developed through the use of red flags on the desks, deli numbers, or names on the board. Students should be encouraged to ask each other for help (*"Ask three then me"*) and to keep on working while waiting for the teacher.

Areas of the room. There are procedures for each area of the room. Students have to be taught how to use the room appropriately and to keep materials in designated areas.

Art area. May they use any materials? How do they prepare (smocks, newspaper, etc.)? What do they do with finished work? What clean up is expected?

Science area. What procedures are there regarding equipment, experiments in progress, and living things?

Math Manipulatives. How is this area kept organized?

Book area. What are the procedures for treatment of books?

Media center. What equipment, such as computers, video players and audio players, may students use? For how long? What if something does not work?

Writing center. Address use of the pencil sharpener and paper. All writing must be on paper, not on the table or walls. When can the pencil sharpener be used? Is there a one-at-a-time rule?

Wastebasket. The wastebasket also follows the one-at-a-time rule. Students should stand within arm's length of the basket and pick up anything that does not go in. Sometimes the papers in the wastebasket have to be pushed down so it does not overflow.

Teacher's area. May students go there? For what?

Areas outside the classroom. Students need to learn expected behavior to and from school, on the bus, and in the cafeteria and hallways.

Meal time and cafeteria. There need to be procedures for meal time. Students should quickly and efficiently wash their hands and go immediately to the eating area. How do they know where to sit? Do they have a choice or is it assigned? After eating, the students should clean up their own places and help wipe off the table.

Hand washing procedures. Hand washing is one of the most important health habits for the prevention of diseases and one of the first things taught in third world countries. Unfortunately, we have become careless in our own country. Students need to be taught how to turn on the faucet, use liquid soap, thoroughly wash, rinse, and use a paper towel, turning off the water with the paper towel. Students should wash hands before cooking and eating, and after toileting.

Teaching the Procedures

Once the procedures have been decided upon, they have to be taught. Sometimes procedures are put in a policy manual and each student is given a copy to take home. Teaching begins on the first day of school with reminders as needed throughout the year. If students are misbehaving, it may be because they have not learned the behaviors expected of them. Reteaching may be necessary (Evertson, Emmer, Clements, Sanford & Worsham, 1989).

The steps in teaching procedures are as follows:

Describe and **explain** the procedures. What exactly are they? What are examples and nonexamples (the right way and the wrong way)? Many times I have sat in the back of a classroom observing a student teacher describe procedures, and I could not figure out what he or she expected the students to do. It takes skill to develop a well thought out procedure and describe it clearly.

I have found that procedures have to be taught to every age level. I have to teach procedures to my college students, even graduate students. For example, I found them opening potato chip bags and turning pages during the one-minute reflection at the beginning of class. I came to realize that reflective and meditative behavior is missing in American culture, so I began stating clearly what to do with their hands, feet, and mind. I even put the procedure in writing on the syllabus. That is a bit condescending, so I have used other approaches. One is to ask, "How do you feel when people are rustling papers, moving around, and popping gum during a reflection?" There is usually at least one person who reacts with outrage, surprising the others. Finding out that they offend their peers is enlightening to them. Another technique I have used is to make a request: "May I ask a favor of you? The reflection is important to me, and it helps when you sit quietly, without moving around." Another strategy is to thank them after the first reflection. "Thank you for sitting quietly without moving around, rustling pages, opening chips bags, etc. I really appreciate the reflective attitude you have shown."

Demonstrate the procedure. The teacher takes on the role of a student and shows or acts out the procedure.

Role play the procedure. The class watches while selected students volunteer to demonstrate the appropriate behavior.

Rehearse and **practice** (drill). The teacher sets up drills where the procedure is practiced by everyone.

Give **feed back**. The teacher compliments students when they follow the procedures. Students learn to compliment each other, either out loud or in writing. They may clap or cheer for each other. The group can motivate individuals to behave well.

There might be a group incentive system where there is a class reward when everyone follows the procedures. For example, they may all choose a reward such as "hanging out" for five minutes at the end of the period, or they may vote to have a joke telling session. "Marble in the Jar" is another group incentive system. Whenever the teacher sees a procedure followed well by the whole class, a marble is placed in a jar. When the jar is full, there is a class treat. Another group incentive activity is where the teacher writes a letter on the chalk board when the whole class is following the procedures. As letters are added, they spell "pop corn party" or "ice cream party." Frederick Jones (1987) suggests that the teacher buy a stop watch and keep it clearly visible to the class. If a student stops following the procedure, the teacher starts the stop watch and deducts that time for the whole class from the special activity. A group incentive makes use of positive peer pressure as students cue each other to "be quiet, hurry up and sit down, or stop talking." Students help and care for each other. The advantage of a group incentive is that everyone works together and keeps each other on task. Everyone also shares the benefit. External rewards such as ice cream cones or bowls of popcorn are not going to develop character, and if students are cruel to each other, the group incentive system needs to be changed or discontinued.

Procedures and Character Building

Students are learning to develop good habits of behavior, to keep the classroom community running smoothly and efficiently, and use time wisely. When procedures are followed, less time is wasted, and there is more time for participatory learning.

Of course, the teacher also must model time management skills. Jacob Kounin (in Edwards, 1997) found that ineffective teachers were lacking in organizational skills and time management; students were expected to sit and wait; transitions took too long; the teacher's pacing was either so slow students were bored or so fast they couldn't keep up. When teachers show good time management skills, they are showing respect for student time. Having students wait in lines for long periods says "I have no respect for your time," and it's not surprising that students take the same attitude. The goal is that everyone will use time wisely.

Relationships among Students

Relationships begin with learning each others' names, getting acquainted, working together, and building friendships and a sense of community (Charney, 1992). The classroom is a good environment for developing peer relationships. Many children with special needs are now in regular classrooms. This form of **inclusion** can be beneficial if students are encouraged to help each other, respect everyone, and focus on the strengths of others. Students can learn to understand, appreciate, and admire people with learning differences and challenges.

Name recognition

There is evidence that students treat each other better when they know each others' names, because they begin to see each other as people. Students can make their own name tags which are later used for drawing names out of a hat. Each student might study the history of his or her name, what it means, and why it was chosen, and share this through a name board or poster which is also used for decoration in the classroom. Many names stand for character traits. For example, Lance means "proud warrior." Nicknames can be discussed. Students should be called by their preferred name. It is important that everyone correctly pronounce the names of others, including non-English names. This is part of building respect for diversity. Names can be used for acrostics, name searches, and crossword puzzles. The computer can be used for writing a name in different type faces and sizes.

There are name games such as "This is the house that Jack built," in which each person has to state his or her name and put an attribute with it ("I am happy Henry"), the next person has to begin at the beginning, repeating each person's name and adding his or her own ("happy Henry, able Abbie, conscientious Charlie, daring Dan ..."). Another game is to stand in a circle and toss a ball to a peer. Before the ball is tossed, the person's name must be spoken. Tom Lickona has his college students greet each other by name and handshake at the beginning of each class.

Get acquainted activities

Another part of relationship building is getting to know each other, seeing each other as human beings with feelings and aspirations. Students can be asked to draw portraits and self-portraits, and write autobiographies and biographies of each other. Students can interview each other for biographical information. The portraits and bio sketches can be put on the bulletin board. Students try to remember who is who and some interesting thing about that person. Last year I brought my husband's camera to the first class and asked one of the students to take a photograph of each student. Students interviewed each other by asking for their preferred name, the story of their name (first, middle, or last), their hero or heroine, and the character traits the hero/heroine exemplified. This information can be used for a "people scavenger hunt" or a bulletin board (Evertson, Emmer, Clements, Sanford, & Worsham, 1989).

A "television" interview can be conducted using a microphone and speaker. "Ten questions" can be adapted to "five questions." One student is chosen, and five people can ask him or her questions. If a student does not want to answer, he or she says, "Pass."

The teacher might write questions for each page of a student-made book. Each page has a short bio sketch on one student, stating name, date of birth, age, family members, interests, abilities, and values. Riddles and guessing games are played using the information generated. Class surveys and statistics can be collected and displayed in graph form. For example, a student may ask, "What is the most important character trait?" and tabulate the results.

In some classes like Carol Barron's Somersworth Middle School in New Hampshire, there is a "student of the week," based on birthday. The student brings pictures, mementos, parents, siblings, other family members, and pets to school. Students write "I like" statements about the student of the week as a way of focusing on positives.

"Show and tell" is a time-honored way of getting to know each other. Each person brings in an object that represents his or her interest or values. These are shared with others. Students are also encouraged to share news about what is happening in their lives.

The more students get to know each other and see others as human beings with feelings, the less they will want to victimize each other.

Friendship Building

Classroom activities provide a foundation for friendships. Many years ago I took a college class in which each person had to go up front and talk about him or herself. One of the other students interested me. Later she told me she had felt the same way when I presented. We sought each other out, became friends and roommates, and developed a friendship that outlasted our college days.

There should be time for students to work together and get to know each other without direct teacher involvement. The easiest way is "pair and share." Students become partners with the person next to them, and they work on a project such as a get acquainted interview together. The results are often shared with the whole group. Other friendship-building activities include playing a board or card game, putting a puzzle together, using an area of the room such as the computer or science table together, paired reading where they read to each other, role plays, case studies, project work, and free time to talk.

Unity of Spirit: A Sense of Togetherness

There are activities for developing "class spirit" or "esprit de corps." A class may make a poster for the door, choose a class name (rather than the last name of the teacher), a class logo, mascot, bird, flower, tree, motto, or song. Singing, dancing, creative movement and group recitation are wonderful ways to establish togetherness.

Sociologists describe the rituals that bring a culture together. The teacher more often calls them "routines." A short, meaningful poem, creed, or pledge recited in unison each morning, an inspiring song sung, and a special departure ritual are daily rituals. A Friday afternoon treat might be a weekly ritual. Celebration of the first snow is an example of a yearly ritual. These rituals bring a class together.

Each class has its own story. The class timeline, photo album, video tape, or daily news story help keep track of shared memories. When I taught first and second grade, each day ended with a ten minute ritual where I asked, "What was different or special about today?" I wrote the students' exact words and typed them out as a weekly newsletter. One year the students took turns writing the newsletter. A copy was kept in a notebook in the class library for students to read.

Moral Exercises Fostering Student Interaction with Each Other

In moral exercises, students learn by doing: moving, talking, writing, acting, and interacting. Students are making choices and decisions. They are taking initiative and evaluating their work. According to Piaget (1965), children are active learners who construct their own knowledge.

Role Play

In a role play, students are assigned the roles of people involved in a situation. For example, one student is the teacher, another is the student who was late to class, another is a fellow student, another is a parent, and another is the principal. Each person is expected to think of the issue from the point of view of the person he or she represents and to act out that role. A clearly defined standard of virtues is explained first. Each person must state his or her feelings and opinions in light of universal values or virtues. Each is asked to consider his or her behavior in light of a common core of values. Sometimes it is helpful for everyone to take a different role and to look at the situation from another point of view. Role playing is an exercise in moral reasoning and perspective taking.

Case Studies

Students might be asked to examine case studies of realistic but hypothetical situations. The game *Choices* provides many case studies. For example, here are two cards from *Choices:*

Card 1

A friend's mother invites you to a movie. It won't be over until late. You can't reach your parents for permission. Do you go anyway?

Card 2

You are quite certain that your school bus driver drinks liquor from his Thermos while driving. You ask him politely and privately if it is true. He says it isn't. Will you look into it further?

Students make a decision, explain what they would do and why they would do it, and **how their choice would demonstrate a universal value**. They check to see if everyone agrees. If not, the issue is discussed. Sometimes universal values are in conflict. One student may choose honesty, and another, kindness. As students discuss what they would do in light of universal values, they learn to articulate their beliefs, and examine the perspectives of others.

Sometimes case studies are in the form of an ethical dialogue. In the books, *What would you do? A-1* and *B-1* (1989) by Michael Baker, a problem such as this is posed: "Suppose you go into a store to buy a few items. After the cashier adds your items, he/she gives you a total that is about half of what you expected." Baker lists as many as twenty questions to consider in this situation:

Would you ask the cashier if he/she miscalculated? Would you pay the bill and remain silent? Would you pay the bill but comment that the bill is not as much as you expected? Would you do something else? What would you do?

He then adds conditions to the situation,

"What if the cashier is someone you know? Would this change what you would do? What if the cashier seems very sad about something?"

Students go through the exercise and answer each question. They may disagree with each other over the answers. This builds cognitive dissonance and helps them think more clearly. The teacher listens to student answers and asks questions in a Socratic manner so as to guide students toward universal values.

There are many commercially produced board and card games in which students have to make choices or share their opinions. There are also videos in which a moral dilemma is portrayed through a short skit. Students watch the skit and then talk about or role play their solution. There are also open-ended stories. Students decide how the plot will evolve. These exercises give an opportunity to practice moral decision making with attention to universal values and real life situations.

Teachers can create their own vignettes describing moral situations or problems based on real experiences in the classroom. Each vignette is written on a separate card and ends with, "What should they do?" Students discuss their answers.

Debate

In middle school and above, students may be assigned a project such as a debate in which more than one side of an issue is presented. A debate team usually consists of 2-6 members on each side. One team researches one side and other researches the opposite. This helps their perspective-taking ability. Often the debate is about moral issues such as liberalism versus conservatism, capital punishment, the justice of war, capitalism versus socialism, or nuclear power or environmental engineering. One side speaks at a time for a specified amount of time. They are then allowed two chances to rebut each other's arguments.

The schedule for a debate is as follows:

> Presentation by the Pros (10 minutes)
> Presentation by the Cons (10 minutes)
> Rebuttal by the Pros (5 minutes)
> Rebuttal by the Cons (5 minutes)
> Rebuttal by the Pros (3 minutes)
> Rebuttal by the Cons (3 minutes)

Cooperative Learning

Cooperative learning is being used in many classrooms. Teachers group children heterogeneously so that they work together toward a common goal. Each person has a role or responsibility for contributing to the learning process. Typically roles are: leader, recorder, time keeper, encourager. There are many different forms of cooperative learning. I plan at least one cooperative learning exercise in each 75 minute college class. In order for cooperative learning to work, students need to help and support each other (Dishon and O'Leary, 1994). **Character education is an essential part of cooperative learning** because, in order for it to be beneficial, students have to treat each other with respect, accepting and respecting differences, and learning when to and when not to help each other. They have to learn to take responsibility for themselves and others, to be tolerant of different abilities and disabilities, and to have conversations in which respect is shown to everyone. The use of "learning pairs" or the "buddy system," peer tutoring, and mentoring increase helping and sharing skills. Students need to be told when to do their own work, when to collaborate with others, and how to give credit to others when they work together.

Class Meeting

There are ways to involve the whole class democratically in a large group exercise. One method is the **class meeting** (sometimes called *community meeting, morning meeting, circle time, magic circle* or *friendship ring*), in which students have an opportunity to converse as a class (Glasser, 1975). In a class meeting, the students and teacher sit in a circle. Each person is given a chance to speak, going around the circle in order at least once. No interruptions are allowed, and if a student does not wish to speak, he or she can say "pass." After a person has spoken, others may ask questions to clarify what was said. The teacher and students listen respectfully to each other. The rules are: no putdowns, insults, or name calling; address issues and ideas rather than personalities; and courtesy and respect should be shown (Schmidt, Friedman & Marvel, 1992). A class meeting should be held on the first day of school, because if students talk on the first day, they will be more apt to participate throughout the whole year. The teacher explains the purpose of the class meeting and the rules. Being listened to with respect can have a positive effect on behavior. The first class meeting may be to share what they learned that summer, what they hope to learn this year, what conditions each needs in order to learn, or what virtues will be needed in the classroom. The teacher chooses one question and each student answers it. Often there is a recorder who takes notes on the chalkboard, overhead or piece of paper.

In Ruth Charney's book *Teaching children to care* (1992), she describes the value of class meetings for building a sense of community, getting to know each other, greetings, sharing news, helping each other, planning and solving problems, and working together. Sometimes the class meeting is a "bull session" for talking about anything the students have on their minds. Or it may be used for reviewing what students know, want to know, or learned about a particular subject. It is a forum for meaningful exchange and information gathering. Students hear what others think and express their own opinions openly. It creates a safe environment for expressing feelings and for discussing and resolving issues. Students can learn to communicate their feelings in an appropriate way. The teacher models listening respectfully.

Open Mike

If there is no issue that needs to be resolved but students have many things to say, an "open mike" may be called. These have become popular in high schools. An Open Mike means anyone can go to the microphone and say anything about anything. There may be a time limit. Students support the speakers through clapping and cheering.

Class Governance

The teacher looks for ways to turn the governance of the classroom over to the students. This does not happen all at once but is scaffolded in a way that students can handle successfully.

For example, the teacher may use a rotating schedule and have students give a one or two minute homily each morning. Each student may be asked to write a student code of ethics. A class meeting or open mike can be used for developing a classroom code of ethics, creed, or mission statement.

Procedures can be developed by students through a committee approach. Each committee or small group drafts a proposed procedure. For example, one committee may study "lining up." After watching the class and other classes, and talking with the teacher and other teachers, the committee recommends a procedure for lining up. The recommendation becomes a warrant article for "town meeting" or an action item for "parliament." The whole class studies the recommendation, discusses it, and votes.

There may be committees that deal with specific areas. For example, there might be a custodial, cafeteria, or library committee. Some committees are *ad hoc*, meaning that they are formed for a specific purpose and are disbanned when done. There might be an ad hoc Halloween committee. Antelope Trails Elementary School in Colorado has the following committees: the planning committee, which plans special days and events; the lost and found committee; the helping committee, which keeps the environment clean and orderly; and the reaching out committee, which plans community service projects. Students can plan advocacy campaigns for moral issues. A steering committee assigns tasks to others and launches the project.

Executive Structure

The class may elect officers: president, vice president, secretary, and treasurer. This may be varied with titles such as mayor, governor, or prime minister. These take responsibility for keeping the classroom running smoothly. They may plan social activities, as well as class projects. Their duties and obligations should be clear and in writing.

The teacher usually begins the year by modeling—demonstrating how the various chores are done. Once students accept responsibility, the teacher becomes a coach, advisor, facilitator, and even substitute. Teachers who are used to taking all responsibility worry that students may make poor decisions. If that happens, the teacher can choose one of the following courses of action:

a) Exercise the power of veto. It should be made clear in advance that the teacher has this power and why.

"As the professional educator responsible for this classroom in the eyes of the law, I cannot agree to that. Think of something I could agree to."

b) State his or her opinion why it won't work, but let them try it if they insist. The teacher would do this only when failure would not be detrimental to the children's welfare.

"I think you may regret making this decision. Are you sure you want to do this? Let me tell you what might happen."

c) Stay out of it and let the students experience unharmful failure. After trying a plan that doesn't work, the teacher might call a new class meeting and say, *"How do you feel about your decision?"* Each student expresses an opinion, and the class decides how to revise its plan.

Class Constitution

Writing a class constitution is a moral exercise in which students study their country's or state's constitution, the Magna Carta or Mayflower Compact, and then write their own. There may be many drafts before they finalize the rules and regulations for their classroom. When the class constitution is completed, it can be copied onto a poster and each student signs it. The constitution becomes a contract to which all are committed. Students can learn about keeping their word and following through with agreed upon rules. It could be displayed next to a poster of the U.S. Constitution.

Class Goal Setting

Rather than form rules, the class may choose character traits as goals or ideals toward which to strive. Students may be asked to first write down, then share in the class meeting, the virtues and goals they are striving toward. Common goals are posted for all to see.

Goals can be stated in the form of the Golden Rule or some other motto. They may be part of an acronym or short poem. They should be short (no more than five), positive, observable, and reasonable. They should be displayed for all to see and refer to. They should cover student action toward each other and the teacher, as well as property and their work. They should also cover problem areas. Because they are guiding principles, they do not have to be specific.

Examples of goals:

- *Classroom 1:* I promise to do my best to be respectful and responsible.
- *Classroom 2:* Be kind. Be respectful. Work hard.
- *Classroom 3:* I am safe. I am a friend. I solve problems.
- *Classroom 4:* Trustworthiness, Respect, Responsibility, Caring, Fairness

Two third grade team teachers in Plymouth, New Hampshire, brought their classes together and asked the students to brainstorm words or phrases that describe a good person (see the exercise at the end of chapter 2). One teacher scribed (wrote as spoken) the list on newsprint, and everyone read it together in unison. The list was edited by combining words that were alike and taking out duplicates. The next day each character trait was at the top of a piece of newsprint. If the virtue was "polite," students were asked to describe behaviors that show politeness. These were also recorded and left hanging on the walls. At the end of the week, students read the lists together, and the teachers asked if anything had been forgotten. A few items were added. Then students were asked to assess themselves: "How did you do this week?"

Classroom Rules

Some teachers choose to have class rules rather than goals. Goals state the ideals. Rules prescribe action. For example, if kindness is a goal, *Be kind to others* is a rule. *Stand in line quietly* is a procedure or strategy.

Students should be helped to value rules and procedures as advantageous, meeting personal and academic needs. Following rules and procedures is one way of contributing to the group. President Bill Clinton, at the second White House conference on character said, "I am convinced that there are millions of Americans who get up every day and do the right thing." Students need to develop law-abiding habits of behavior. Following rules and procedures is good preparation.

Commitment to the rules is needed from all parties, shown through raising hands, an auditory vote, or signing their names to a pledge, contract or agreement.

Consequences

There is a basic understanding that rules and procedures can be followed or broken, that there are consequences to following and breaking them. There is a chain effect, outcome, result, consequence, or benefit to each moral action. Using schematic mapping, students can explore the consequences of an action. For example:

Action→ negative consequence

Name calling → hurt feelings → another put down→ anger →
broken friendship→ friends take sides→ classmates uncomfortable→
harder to concentrate → less learning takes place → less trust → less
cooperation→ lower self esteem.

Action → positive consequence

Student greets peer cordially → greeted back → strengthen friendship → strengthen community → positive feelings of happiness →
more confidence → more risk taking → better able to learn.

Shure and Spivack (1988) developed the "What would happen if" game to help students predict consequences.

Town Meeting

One form of processing governmental action is the "town meeting." Issues, called *warrant articles*, are put on an agenda (a large piece of newsprint or corner of the chalk board) by anyone in the class. One person is the moderator, and anyone can speak for or against the warrant articles. When discussion is over, a vote is taken, either by hand or ballot.

Class Parliament

In this approach, the class uses *Robert's rules of order* (1907) for following parliamentary procedure. It elects a chair, vice chair, and secretary. The chair accepts motions from the floor, which must be seconded and then opened for discussion. When the discussion is over, a vote is taken. The secretary keeps minutes and prepares an agenda ahead of time. Sometimes one person, called the *parliamentarian,* is placed in charge of studying *Robert's rules* and making sure procedures are followed correctly.

Press Conference

When students have a lot of questions about a specific policy or event, the teacher may call a "press conference." After giving a brief statement, the teacher opens it up for members of the class to ask questions.

Student Planning

One important concept in character education is teaching students to take control of their own behavior, be responsible, and work together within the community of the classroom. Students can set goals, strive to reach those goals, and evaluate their work afterwards.

A planning process helps them be responsible, thoughtful, and organized decision makers. David Weikart (Hohmann, Banet, & Weikart, 1979) developed a model program called the High Scope approach, wherein young children learn to plan what they are going to do and how they will do it. It is called the Plan, Do, Review cycle.

Planning Skills Can Be Taught.

Planning is helping students be responsible, thoughtful, organized decision makers.

> The steps in the planning model are as follows:
> > Set goal
> > Plan
> > Work
> > Represent (optional)
> > Recall (review, reflect)
> > Evaluate

First, students are given time to set goals and plan strategies for reaching those goals. They are encouraged to think ahead about what materials they will use, with whom they will work, and what they will do. They make their own plans, which are approved by the teacher before proceeding.

Goal Setting

Goal setting has been covered in other parts of this book. Each student needs to have vision, ideals, and goals to strive toward.

Planning

The teacher might ask, "What do you plan to do to reach your goal?" At the beginning of the year, plans are brief. Later students may become so skillful that they make lists or outlines, or draw a picture or blueprint. Student plans are written down and kept to show their development. Planning is a vehicle for turning goals into action, idealism into behavior, moral knowing into moral doing.

Sometimes students make unrealistic plans like, "I'm going to find a place for all the homeless." The teacher picks out a key feature and helps the student make a doable plan by saying, "You are going to do something to help the homeless."

At the beginning of the year students listen to each others' plans and learn from them. One or two skillful planners can model for the rest of the class. Later, as planning becomes more routine, there are several ways to speed up the process. Students may write their plans. Group plans in which students work together are encouraged. It is possible to start the day with planning as they enter the room. They could be asked to talk with their parents and bring their goal and plan with them. Some teachers have a meeting where each student describes aloud his or her plan. Other teachers develop planning sheets which students fill out in writing. Planning includes "have tos" or requirements (assigned by the teacher) as well as choices or electives determined by the student.

Work Time

During work time, students carry out the plans they have made. If they get sidetracked and are not carrying out their plans, the teacher reminds them of the original plan and asks if they want to make a new one. Students are not forced to stick with their original plan, but they must follow a plan. If students wander around the room, the teacher might say, "Are you following your plan?" Many behavior problems are due to poor planning ability. Frederick Jones (1987) studied classrooms to find that there was massive time wasting, sometimes as much as 40 percent of class time. There were two types of behavior which caused this: 80 percent was off-task talking and 19 percent was walking around or "fooling around." Planning helps students stay on task and focused. There are many questions which can be used guiding students' planning. Here is a sampling of typical questions teachers have asked. Once they understand the process, most teachers use their own words, and ask only one question for each step in the planning process.

Planning

GOAL(S)
What goal are you reaching toward?
What character trait do you want to show?
What is important to you?

PLAN
Where will you go?
How will you reach your goal?
What strategies will you use?
What is your plan?
What do you plan to do?
What are you going to do today?
Have you decided what you are going to do?
What would you like to do today?
How about showing me something you will work with.
Point to the area where you plan to work.
Can you see something you would like to do?
What are you going to use?
What materials will you use?
What are you going to work with?
What else will you do?
Who will work with you?

WORK
Are you following your plan?
How is your plan going?
Is your plan working?
Have you had to change your plan?
Do you need to change your plan?

REPRESENT (optional)
Would you like to tell me about what you did? (same as *recall*)
Would you like to draw a picture of that?
Could you write down what you did?
Let's take a picture of that!
Show me what you did (nonverbal demonstration).
Let's make a model of what you did.
Let's video tape your play.
Why don't you tell about it on this cassette player?

RECALL

What was your plan? How did you follow it?
How did you do that?
What did you do today?
Describe what you did.
Tell us how we could do what you did.

EVALUATE

Did your plan work?
How might it have worked better?
What worked best?
What did you like doing?
What are you proud of?
If you did it tomorrow, what would you do again?
What problems did you have? How did you solve them?
Is there anything that disappointed you about your plan?
What could you have done?
What will you probably do next time?
What do you wish you had done?
How could you have done this differently?
Did you do what you wanted to do?
Could you have done it better? How?
What is your favorite part of this?
What did you like the most about what you did?
What do you think is the best part?
What needs to be fixed?

The teacher listens to and approves plans, keeps records, and serves as a resource, providing information that might influence the students' choices. Once the plan is in place, the teacher cues students by saying, "Are you following your plan? What did you plan to do? Are you doing it? How is your plan coming? Is what you are doing right or wrong?" During work time, the teacher observes, assists, questions, supports, encourages, and describes with genuine interest students' planning skills. When they are having problems with their plans, the teacher helps them think things through.

After carrying out a plan, there is value in representing it in another medium. This could be done in several ways. Students may describe verbally or nonverbally what they did. They may draw a picture or write about it. Sometimes a photograph or video is made.

Recall

It is important that students reflect on what they did. This is called **recall**, results, or *Review and Evaluation*. It may be done informally as they finish, at a final large group session, or outside of school time. There is a checklist in the appendix for using the planning sequence in the classroom.

First Day

The goal of the first day is to begin structuring a moral community. The first day of school is the most important for getting a character education program started. *(For teachers who are reading this during the school year, there are many "first days": the beginning of each week, after holidays and school vacations, and the beginning of a new year.)* The teacher begins to establish a relationship with each student and students begin to get to know each other and to feel excitement about being part of a new class. Moral direction is given, the initial procedures are explained, and moral exercises are begun. These exercises will be used for building the classroom governance structure. The curriculum is also foreshadowed.

What Must Be Covered on the First Day

Arrival

Students of all ages need eye contact, often a handshake, and a smile as they are greeted warmly at the door. There should be name tags. They need to hear their names pronounced correctly, and they need to see the teacher's enthusiasm in meeting them.

Procedures

There are procedures that must be taught as soon as possible, such as what to do at arrival, what to do in case of an emergency, and how to behave during teacher-led instruction.

Room and School Tour

Students are usually given a visual tour of the room. If the teacher has already determined the procedure for use of each area, it is explained, demonstrated, and role played. If the procedures are going to be determined by the students, an overview is given.

Schedule

The schedule, which is often posted, is explained so that students can follow the rhythm of the day or class period.

Introduction of Teacher and Students

Students learn each others' and the teacher's names. Games and activities are used for this.

Get acquainted Activity

Get acquainted activities are used to help students learn about each other. Interviews, drawings, "people scavenger hunts," and other activities are used so that students get to know each other better.

Friendship Building

There is an activity in which students interact with each other in small groups. They are given a task to plan and complete together. A character-building activity might be to ask them to describe a good person or suggest class goals. They may make decorations for the classroom. During this time, the teacher catches up on administrative activities and circulates around the room, listening and keeping students on task.

Initiate Group Feeling

The teacher initiates a sense of community or togetherness through music, discussion, choosing a class name, or some other community-building activity.

Class Governance

Students begin to think about how the classroom should be run. They may be asked to reflect silently and fill out a questionnaire or there may be a whole class discussion.

First Day: Goals and Plan

Begin relationship with teacher.
Build friendships among students.
Develop a sense of community.
Become familiar with the environment.
Begin governing structure.
Set up procedures and schedule.

1. **Greeting**: See each individual as person.
   name, eye contact, smile
2. **Friendship Circle**: Learn names of others.
3. **Introductions**: "This is my friend..."
4. **Exhortation**: Teacher's goals
5. **Personal Goals**
6. **Shared Goals**: Common goals
7. **Visualize Goals**: Campaign begins
   Campaign button, t-shirt, hat, sign, poster, commercial, speech, slogan, motto, bumper sticker, cheer, promise, bulletin board, song.
8. **Room Tour**: Shared spaces related to common goals:
   bulletin boards, walls, door, chalk board, pencil sharpener, waste basket, materials
9. **School Tour**: Shared spaces and common goal: Choose a school project "to make the school better."
10. **Schedule and Curriculum:** Foreshadow learning

Content Learning

The content of the curriculum should be introduced or foreshadowed. Students may read a short poem or essay, set their own subject area goals, or skim textbooks.

First Day Activities

Check List:

___ Motto of the day is posted
___ Introduce self and students
___ Give room tour and procedures for areas
___ Get acquainted activity
___ Goal setting exercise (personal)
___ Introduce class meeting
___ Goal setting exercise (class)
___ Present governing structure (who is in charge of what)
___ Present procedures for specific needs
___ Initiate sense of community
___ Friendship-building activity
___ Room decorations (who makes what)
___ Story (piece of literature)
___ Quality time with individual students

Summary

Beginning on or before the first day of school, students can take responsibility for their classroom. In order for them to be invested, the teacher carefully builds a positive relationship between students. Expectations are made clear through procedures. Procedures need to be carefully thought out ahead of time and clearly explained. If students are misbehaving, it may be because the procedures are inappropriate or not explained well.

Governing structures are put in place. Students who take responsibility for their own learning are building character. When students have set their own goals, they are less apt to waste time. Disorganized students lose homework, forget to study for tests, and generally do poorly in school due to lack of planning ability. On the other hand, skilled planners stay focused, keep a list of homework assignments, write assignments on a calendar, and are well organized. They are successful in school because they have used planning skills.

Teaching students to plan is an important skill. Each day there is a Plan, Do, Review cycle. This teaches students to take charge of their own learning, organize themselves, and reflect on what they have learned. The teacher plans open-ended activities in which students can use their planning skills and guides students through the planning process by asking key questions.

Exercises

These exercises are written for teachers who wish to form or strengthen their classroom as a moral community.

1. Design a daily schedule including the Plan, Do, Review cycle.
2. Write out the procedures for:
   - arrival
   - large group time
   - planning time
   - clean up time
   - outdoor time
   - meal time
   - rest or quiet time
   - departure
   - lining up
   - manners with visitors
   - toileting
   - getting a drink
   - obtaining help from the teacher
   - each area of the room
3. Discuss people you know who were poor or efficient planners.
4. Visit a High Scope classroom and use the checklist for planning in the Appendix.
5. Write a schedule for the first day.
6. Plan a class governance system.

CHAPTER 6

Moral Correction

DISCIPLINE, GUIDANCE, AND BEHAVIOR MANAGEMENT

This chapter examines ways to work with misbehavior (often called *off-task* or *inappropriate* behavior). It provides strategies for guiding students who have made poor choices and done something wrong.

This chapter follows the premise outlined in chapter 1, that behavior is produced by character, and character by vision. A great deal of misbehavior can be prevented by having a compelling vision (see chapter 1), ethical leadership (chapter 3), a moral climate (chapter 4), and a moral community (chapter 5).

However, even when the desire for good character is there, acquiring it comes through a gradual process of development and learning, sometimes learning from one's own mistakes. Self-discipline, or self-control, and prudence, or wise judgment, come from experience.

This chapter provides many techniques for using misbehavior as an opportunity for character education.

Requesting Behavior

Cueing

"Teachers have eyes in the back of their heads" is a common adage. This means they are constantly on the alert (Kounin, in Edwards, 1997). They position themselves where they can see students, even when it is peripherally. Overhead projectors are better than chalk boards because the teacher can face the class while writing. When talking to an individual student or a visitor at the door, the teacher still faces the class. The reason for watching is to learn about behavior patterns (what students tend to do) and to cue behavior.

Nonverbal cueing is the first level of correcting misbehavior (Canter & Canter, 1992). It may be through **eye contact** ("the look"), **gestures** such as a finger to the lips for being quiet, **facial expressions** that show approval or disapproval, **physical touch** such as a hand on the shoulder (used prudently and never with students who show discomfort), **proximity** (moving nearer the student), or **signals** such as a flick of the lights. Feedback through nonverbal expressions of disappointment and approval are the mildest form of correction.

If the student does not correct his or her behavior when a nonverbal cue is given, the teacher moves to the next level, **non-directive verbal cueing**. The voice is used in a positive way to give a **reminder** such as "Remember, we are showing respect to everyone," a **hint** such as "Goal #1," a **question** like "What character trait should you be showing right now?", a **challenge** like "Who can show respect for others by keeping quiet?", or an "**I message**" such as "I need you to show respect by working without talking." The teacher does not make negative statements like "Stop that," "Don't or "Never." Direct commands given to individual students who are misbehaving may evolve into open confrontations. It is unfortunate that many teachers call out the names of misbehaving students in order to bring them back on task. There are times when we use a student's name to get his or her attention. However, a person's name is a positive thing and should usually be used for positive, rather than negative attention. Reminders, hints, questions, challenges, and "I messages" are more appropriate verbal cues.

Cueing is a guidance technique used to "nip misbehavior in the bud," before it actually happens or as it starts. When teachers are on the alert and know their students well, they can often predict a misbehavior. For example, a student may lift a hand to push someone, or there may be a gleam in the eye and furtive glances. A look from the teacher is enough to remind the student to behave well.

Verbal Communication: Guided Listening

If cueing is not working or the misbehavior has already occurred, the teacher uses a different strategy called *guided listening* (Gordon, 1974). He or she asks questions to better understand the student's point of view. For example, here are three potentially misunderstood situations. In the first, Dee poked Mimi with a pencil. In the second, Jo knocked another student down. In the third Juan has another student in an arm lock. The teacher who uses guided listening does not jump to conclusions but asks, "What are you trying to do?" (What character trait should you be showing? What is your goal? What are you trying to accomplish?) In guided listening, the teacher listens to the students' point of view, using words like "Tell me what happened. What went wrong? Why did you do that?" Eye contact and body language should convey this message: "I am truly listening to what you have to say."

Guided listening is not easy for classroom teachers because there are other distractions. Many times I have watched a teacher ask a question, but become distracted by other things happening in the room, and never really listen to the student's answer.

The teacher may request a private conference in a corner of the room or hall, or after class. At the conference the teacher asks one or more of these questions: "What did you do? What did you do wrong? What character trait did you show or not show? How is this behavior helping you? How should you have behaved differently?" (Glasser, 1985, 1969)

Many times students can correct their own misbehavior if they just have someone to listen to them.

Some teachers use journals in which students can write out their thoughts and feelings. The teacher can read them after school.

Door Openers

Effective listeners do not react to the first words spoken, but try to get the full picture. Here are typical **door openers** to promote communication:

- *Would you like to talk?*
- *Really? Oh? I'd like to hear about it.*
- *Tell me more. Tell me about it.*
- *I'm interested in your point of view.*
- *Tell me the whole story. I'm listening.*
- *It sounds like you've got something to say about this. This seems important to you.*

Door openers let people know that what they have to say is respected, that their ideas are worth listening to, and most of all, that the teacher cares.

The students in the examples above might respond, "I was trying to get a pencil." "I wanted to go through the door." "He took my paper. I want it back."

Active Listening

After listening intently, the teacher does not rebut, refute, or put down the student's words, but instead summarizes what the student said: "You feel the only way you could get your pencil was to grab it quick." "You pushed her because you needed to get through the door." "You are trying to get your paper back." Statements beginning with, "You think," "You feel," or "You wish," are used to identify and name the student's feelings and goals. Effective listening is not parroting—repeating verbatim what the student said. It is summarizing and rephrasing, as well as figuring out the underlying message. For example, if a student says, "I hate her," an effective listener might respond, "It sounds as though you are upset about something she did."

When children tattle, the teacher uses effective listening, saying, "Did that upset you? How did you feel when he did that? What did you say to him?" The teacher might say to the other student, "Did you hear what she said? How does she feel about what you did? What could you do about it?"

According to Thomas Gordon (1974), too often adults resist students' negative feelings and behavior by ordering, directing, commanding, warning, threatening, preaching, lecturing, judging, criticizing, disagreeing, blaming, name calling, ridiculing, or shaming. When feelings are rejected, students stop communicating and feel unaccepted, inadequate, defensive, and resentful. When feelings are suppressed, they get stronger and perhaps appear in different form. When they are recognized and accepted, students can begin to deal with the situation.

I Messages

The teacher communicates his or her feelings as well and expects to be listened to with respect. Gordon suggests that the teacher use "I messages," beginning statements with "I need" or "I feel." Students can learn to become sensitive to the needs and feelings of the teacher, as well as to those of each other.

Basic Needs

Sometimes misbehavior is an attempt to meet a basic need. For example, everyone needs attention, social recognition, love and belonging, power, autonomy, a sense of useful contribution to the group, justice, and fun (Dreikurs, 1968; Glasser, 1992). The teacher seeks to determine what basic need the student is trying to meet and may state it out loud: It seems that you want me to notice you *(attention)*. Could it be that you wanted everyone to notice you? Could it be that you think I don't like you *(love and belonging)*? Could it be that you want to be in charge *(power)*? Did you think something was unfair *(justice)*? Were you trying to have fun? The student will usually show by body language or verbal response when the teacher has identified the true reason for the misbehavior. Once the basic need is identified, the teacher helps the student find more appropriate ways to meet that need.

Sometimes misbehavior is due to poor scheduling. When students have to sit for long periods of time, they get restless. When they are required to wait and do nothing, they get bored. When they are expected to be quiet for too long, they tend to make noise, and they can handle structured activities only for short periods. In each of these situations, basic needs are being ignored.

Sometimes the behavior is caused by an underlying need that is deeper than a classroom teacher can fix. Some children misbehave because of inner hurts due to abuse, neglect, parental divorce, a father's absence, mental illness, sexual activity, substance use, having committed a crime, family trauma, or crisis. The teacher can rarely deal with these kinds of things directly, but when they are interfering with learning, a referral can be made to the guidance department and appropriate community resource organizations.

Moral Reasoning

Some teachers focus on developing moral reasoning. Students are given hypothetical case studies. Using ethical reasoning, the teacher questions: What is the situation? What should be done? Why? Students describe what should have been done in the light of character traits. The teacher might ask, "What character trait should be shown? How could you show that character trait? How do you want to be treated by others? What should happen if someone mistreats someone else? What should happen if you have not done your best work?

In his book, *How good people make tough choices* (1995), Rushworth Kidder describes nine steps for ethical decision making:

1. Awareness: *Recognize that there is a moral issue.*
2. Actor: *Whose dilemma is this?*
3. Facts: *Gather all the relevant details.*

4. Right/Wrong: *Test for wrongdoing.*
   a. Legal test: *Is it legal?*
   b. Stench test: *Would people say this stinks?*
   c. Front page test: *Would I want my decision printed on the front page of the local paper?*
   d. Mom test: *Would my mom approve?*
5. Right/right: *Determine paradigms. What universal values are in conflict?*
6. Resolution: *How can we resolve this?*
7. Trilemma: *Is there a third way out?*
8. Decision: *Decide what to do.*
9. Reflection: *Revisit the decision later.*

Kohlberg's Stages and Correction

Both Piaget and Kohlberg believed that there are developmental stages of moral reasoning. Kohlberg built on Piaget's work and identified six stages. Every stage describes something common to human beings of all ages. For example, all human beings would like to avoid punishment (stage one), gain material rewards (stage two), be given praise and approval (stage three), see law and order (stage four), participate in community life (stage five) and believe in universal values (stage six). The idea is that although a person may use the thinking of many stages, most independent decisions cluster in one stage, or two adjacent stages when a person is in transition.

Often people ask for a correlation of ages and stages. Kohlberg found no strong correlation, that there are adults operating in stage one, and that in order to be in stages five or six, a person must achieve formal operational thinking (usually around puberty). Piaget's stages have been both verified and questioned.

I have found Kohlberg's stages helpful in correcting misbehavior, because they explain motivation (What motivates this child to be good?). That motivation can be harnessed through a behavior management plan which matches moral development. I have been using six behavior management systems for many years. Recently I have found that they fit nicely when organized around Kohlberg's stages. Kohlberg himself did not design them. However, his stages offer a structure for organizing these systems and relating them to moral development.

Educators are always encouraging students to progress by moving up to the next stage. "Plus one" challenges have been effective in supporting development. Teachers may ask why they would use stage five exercises when their students are stage two thinkers. My explanation is that we want students to be able to operate at higher levels, so we introduce those levels. Here Vygotsky's ideas are helpful. He refers to two levels of learning: the **natural level** used for independent thought and discovery learning, and the **cultural level** induced by good teaching which he called scaffolding. Vygotsky believed that education leads development. This means teachers can introduce higher level concepts and teach them through scaffolding before a child discovers or internalizes them independently. It would explain why teachers can use high level exercises with young children. In fact don't be surprised if you see a kindergarten teacher using stage five exercises successfully! On the other hand, when a higher level system does not seem to be working, teachers tend to move back to a more primitive one, which closer matches the student's natural level.

Stage One: Punishment and Obedience

In the most primitive stage of preconventional reasoning, the motivation for behavior is to avoid **punishment**. Punishment refers to something that causes physical or psychological pain. Sigmund Freud believed the motivation for moral behavior was fear of punishment, anxiety, and guilt. He believed people behave well in order to avoid the anxiety and reduce the tension caused by doing something wrong and that the conscience is the internalized, punitive voice of the parent (Rieff, 1959). Historically, teachers used punishment as the main form of correction.

A teacher from Massachusetts in the 1700s kept track of his discipline for fifty-one years. Here is his summary:

Blows with the cane	911,257
Blows with the rod	124,110
Blows with the ruler	20,989
Blows with the hand	136,715
Blows over mouth	12,235
Boxing of ears	7,905
Rap on head	1,115,800
Blow with book	22,700
Forced to kneel on peas	777

The following is a discipline system from the 1800s:

	Use of switch and whipping post # of lashes
Boys and girls playing together	4
Fight	5
Playing cards	10
Climbing	1 lash for each 3' climbed
Lies	7
Staying out of school	8
Using a nickname	8
Swearing	8
Leaving school without permission	10
Liquor at school	4
Having long fingernails	8
Hollering and whooping on the way home	2
Troubling the writing of others	4
A blot in one's copy book	4

Physical (called *corporal*) punishment is outlawed in most schools today. Although it was called the "rod of correction" there is no empirical evidence that it improved behavior, and there is evidence that it is correlated with aggression (Schultz, Wright, & Schleifer, 1986). It has been found that punishment and power-assertive discipline weaken internal control (Kohn, 1993). For example, I rode on an airplane beside a substitute teacher from Florida. She told me that often the hardest classes to substitute in have the most punitive teachers. The students never establish internal control because the teacher is so controlling. As a result, they misbehave for the substitute.

Psychological punishment if used at all, should be reserved for students who clearly know the expected behavior and show by body language (the glint in the eye) or words such as "I refuse to do what you tell me to" that they intend to be **willfully defiant** (Dobson, 1992). According to Dobson, every teacher should expect to be challenged and tested because there is usually one student in every class who will be defiant. If this defiance is not addressed immediately, he or she will probably act worse. The teacher should respond with confident decisiveness. The student should be removed from the group (or the group should be removed from the situation). The teacher should confront the student using a scolding to elicit sorrow. Sorrow leads to repentance, restitution, and resolution. Dobson points out that punishment is only effective if given in a spirit of love. "Let love be your guide."

Punishment alone does not teach students how to behave. To illustrate this, imagine punishment being used in the teaching of reading. What if each time a student made a mistake, read a word incorrectly, or could not figure out what a word was, the teacher scolded, slammed the book closed, and told the student to put his/her head on the desk? How would this technique help students learn to read? It may be just as ineffective in teaching positive behavior.

Most educators and psychologists believe punishment should be used sparingly, if at all. Teachers who depend on punishment as their primary means of behavior management, even for students who are not willfully defiant, are not supporting character development.

Stage Two: Naive Hedonism or Instrumental Orientation

Kohlberg's second stage is reward-oriented. People in this stage are motivated by material benefits. Behavior modification, a system made popular by B.F. Skinner in the 1970s and '80s, built on this kind of thinking (Martin & Pear, 1996). The teacher was to target a positive behavior and reinforce it through special treats. The reward might be something **tangible** such as money, a trinket or toy, a book, a squirt of perfume, or some other valued but inexpensive item. The reward might be **graphic** such as a sticker, star, seal, rubber stamp, or badge. It could be a **preferred activity**, something the student likes to do such as watch television. It might be a free time pass, a homework pass, a special privilege to go to a certain place or use a valued piece of equipment, computer time, a prized chore or leadership role, being allowed to sit in a different place or with a friend of choice, extra recess, or having a talking period. These rewards are incentives to work toward.

Another reward system is the token economy. Students are given a token, such as a poker chip or a point, for each good behavior. The tokens are turned in like green stamps at the end of the day or week, and a prize is earned. There may be a menu of things to choose from, based on the number of tokens earned. Some teachers set a goal of 100 points (or any designated number) in order to win a prize. Students keep track of the points they earn. The advantage of the token economy is that there is instant recognition (the point), but delayed gratification (the prize). This increases self-control. Sometimes there are rewards such as a certificate. "Gotcha" coupons or merit tickets can be awarded to students who are found performing good deeds. These coupons can be placed in a jar and there may be a weekly drawing for prizes.

While this system is very appealing to stage two thinkers, it can be used with students in any stage who are having a hard time changing a specific behavior. Rewards may provide a jump start toward a necessary habit. For example, many parents give their young children special treats for brushing their teeth. They might use stickers on a chart, flavored toothpaste, a special toothbrush or drinking cup. These help the child form a positive mental image of brushing teeth, but are no longer needed when brushing the teeth becomes a habit. Many adults set goals and plan a reward for themselves when the goal is reached. Weight Watchers uses this principle, and it is scientifically verifiable that behavior can be changed, at least temporarily, through the use of material incentives.

When external rewards are used, they should be things that the students will like and are not harmful (beware of candy). The reward may be set up in the form of a verbal or written contract which goes like this: I_____ (student's name) agree that when I _____(state the positive behavior), I will earn _____(state the reward).

When this system is the primary form of behavior management, it fosters materialism and greed, rather than good character. It weakens internal control (Skinner believed there is no such thing as conscience) because the motivation is for external reinforcement. Another result can be "learned helplessness," wherein students only behave well for external rewards. The goal of character education is forming internal control and habits of behavior guided by the conscience.

In order to avoid students depending on external rewards, teachers use rewards rarely and only when there seems to be no internal motivation. The teacher couples the reward with a social reinforcement, and weans the child from material rewards as quickly as possible.

Stage Three: Social Relationship Perspective — Good Boy, Good Girl

Students in stage three want to be good so significant others will think well of them (social approval). Many teachers use social reinforcement for good behavior. Public recognition or a word in private, positive notes to parents, a notice on the public address system, a handshake from the principal, work displayed on the board, praise from peers and teacher, and formal awards like a citizenship award are all examples of social reinforcement. Some teachers keep blank "character grams" (telegrams) on their desks and jot a quick note of thanks when students have done a good deed. Others give public recognition in front of the whole class. The teacher may mail post cards home saying, "I caught your child doing something right!" Sometimes social rewards are nonverbal, such as a nod, a wink and a smile, a pat on the back, or a high five. It should be clear to the student exactly what behavior earned this praise, and the teacher can call attention to the character trait as well. For example: "You opened the door for me. Thank you, that was kind." "You finished your work. That shows responsibility." Celebrating success and "catching 'em being good" are ways to cheer students on toward displaying good behavior.

Children can learn to give positive comments ("warm fuzzies") to each other and try to reduce the "cold pricklies" (Freed & Freed, 1983). There can be a "compliment patrol," which watches for good deeds and conscious acts of kindness. Having students catch each other being good is doubly effective because it reinforces the virtue in both observer and doer.

One teacher does an activity called the "unique balloon." Each student has a balloon made out of construction paper (or for older students, it might be a real balloon). The other students write positive qualities about that person on the balloon. Another similar activity is the "compliment cape." Each student wears a cape made of newsprint. Others write compliments on the cape. Some classes have a citizen of the month, who is recognized for good deeds and specific virtues. Heidi Rivard, a first grade teacher in Manchester, New Hampshire, picks one child's name out of a hat each morning. The other students give that child compliments, to which the child responds graciously by saying, "Thank you, (name)" to the child who gave the compliment.

Researchers have found that teachers give three times as many disapproving statements as they do approving. Students need positive feedback for appropriate behavior. They need to be given attention when they do what is right.

Sometimes recognition is given for effort rather than success. Or the teacher may reward steps along the way, called **behavioral chaining** or **shaping**.

Stage Four: Law and Order

Stage four thinkers are concerned primarily with rules of the classroom or school. Teachers who set rules and consequences appeal to stage four thinkers (also stage one of Piaget). In assertive discipline, teachers create three to five rules or laws by which the classroom is run. Anyone who breaks a rule must suffer a predetermined negative consequence. Anyone who follows the rules earns a positive consequence. Students learn that their behavior has consequences, hence justice is served.

Unlike punishment, a consequence is not painful or potentially harmful, but it is uncomfortable and something the student does not like. The teacher imposes it in a neutral, nonhostile way by saying, "When you chose this behavior, you chose that consequence." A consequence must be applied consistently and is not removed regardless of excuses. If students argue, the broken record technique is used, wherein the teacher says, "I understand (or I hear you), but when you chose this behavior, you chose that consequence." If the student argues again, the teacher restates, "I understand, but when you chose this behavior, you chose that consequence." At the third round, the consequence is imposed. There is no arguing or discussion of excuses (Canter & Canter, 1992).

Logical consequences are imposed even when a child has shown **childish irresponsibility** (Dreikurs, 1968; Dobson, 1992). For example, children who spill milk must clean it up. If school work is not completed, it must be done during free time. When students break the rules of an area, they have to leave that area for a short period of time. Canter and Canter (1992) predict that good behavior will last two days. They call it the "0024555 syndrome." By the third day there will be two incidents in which students misbehave. If a consequence is not applied, misbehavior will double and continue to increase.

When it is assumed that students will regulate their behavior based on the consequences, this is preconventional thinking (stages one and two). When consequences are seen as a form of justice serving a larger system, this is stage four thinking.

Stage Five: Democratic Negotiation of Laws

Stages Five thinkers believe rules and laws are created and negotiated for the greater common good. Teachers who have class meetings and teach self-governance as described in the previous chapter are preparing students for stage five thinking. Teachers appealing to stage five thinkers ask, "What did you do? Was that the right thing to do? What should you do about it?"

Problem solving, or cognitive behavior modification, is a behavior management system based on stage five thinking. Students are helped to identify the problem, envision a goal, generate and evaluate solutions, make choices and decisions, plan a course of action, and follow through (Crary, 1984; Shure & Spivack, 1974, Shure, 1992). The teacher might ask the student who hurt someone with a pencil, "How could you get your pencil in a way that shows kindness?" To the student who pushed someone, the teacher says, "Is there a better way to get through the door showing courtesy? What character trait could you show right now?" Students generate alternative ways to behave showing good character.

Problem solving skills are taught. The teacher may use large group time to show students how to attack problems. Being able to size up a situation, recognize that there is a problem, and use effective strategies to solve that problem are some of the most important life skills a person can have. Problem solving ability can be improved with guided practice.

The premise of problem solving is that students need to find better behaviors to replace misbehavior. Students need to figure out *how to behave well.*

Steps in Problem Solving
1) **Identify the problem.**
2) **Set a goal.**
3) **Generate solutions and strategies.**
4) **Evaluate strategies showing good judgment.**
5) **Make a decision or plan.**
6) **Implement the plan.**
7) **Evaluate how it went.**

The steps in problem solving are as follows. *(Suggested questions teachers could ask students are italicized.)*

Step 1: Identify the problem.

The problem is?

What's wrong?

What happened?

What is going on here?

Being able to recognize a problem is an important first step. The teacher asks questions to help the student define the problem. If the student believes there is no problem, the teacher can say, "Your behavior is a problem for the rest of the class (or for me)."

Step 2: Set a goal.

What kind of people did we say we want to be?

What character traits are we working on? (Refer to class motto, pledge, or logo.)

While identifying the problem may clarify the negative behavior, goals clarify the positive behavior. They describe what should happen. Goals help develop positive imagery, a powerful regulator of behavior. Too often students who misbehave or are depressed use negative statements like "I am a failure, I am stupid, I'm no good." They see themselves as deprived, defeated, and diseased. Goals help them form positive images and healthy statements about themselves. If students imagine themselves as competent and successful, they are more apt to become so.

Step 3: Generate solutions and strategies.

Think of how you can meet this goal.

What could you do to solve this problem?

How could you solve this problem in a way that is kind, honest, or fair? (Refer to character traits chosen by class.)

What else could you do?

The next step is to generate strategies for reaching the goal and solving the problem. Students should generate at least three to five strategies. The more ideas generated, the better they get. Adults should resist the temptation to suggest solutions. When answers are not forthcoming, the teacher counts to five silently to give them time to think. **Whoever solves the problem owns it**. When a teacher solves the problem, he or she is responsible for the problem and the solution.

Do not evaluate the solutions as they are presented, or students will become discouraged. Their first solutions are usually their worst. Many first solutions suggest physical aggression. The teacher merely says, "What else could you do?"

Step 4: Evaluate strategies showing good judgment.

Is it right or wrong?

Will this show good character?

What character trait would you be showing?

What will happen if you do that?

Will you both be happy?

How will this solution affect you personally?

What will the long-term effect be?

After three to five solutions have been suggested, the next step is to evaluate them. This takes good judgment or prudence. Teachers should resist the temptation to do the evaluating themselves. The teacher may point out discrepancies, contradictions, inconsistencies, and fallacies in student thinking, or give more information that would change the student's mind. Questions such as "why," "how," and "what would happen" are used to help develop good judgment (Shure & Spivack, 1988). All solutions are evaluated against their effectiveness in meeting the goal and the character traits the students agreed to promote.

There are various moral tests used at this step. For example, the Rotary Club asks these four questions:

- Is it truth?
- Is it fair to all concerned?
- Will it be beneficial to all?
- Will it build goodwill and better friendships?

Other evaluative questions are: Is it safe? Is it effective? Is it kind? Is it the right thing to do?

Step 5: Make a decision or plan.

Which solution(s) will you choose?

What do you need to do first?

Then what will you do?

Now the student makes a decision about what to do. Sometimes the decision is put in the form of a contract, which the student and teacher sign. Making a commitment is important. Sometimes ideas can be combined. Many times I ask students to show me through role play what they will do, rather than just tell me. This is guided practice. If necessary, I will have them show me two or three times until I am sure they have learned the new behavior.

Step 6: Implement the plan.

This step involves moral behavior or action, translating "thinking" into "doing." Teacher and peers may watch and use cueing.

Step 7 : Evaluate how it went.

Did you follow your plan?

Are you a better person?

What went well? What was difficult?

Finally comes accountability or evaluation to determine whether the problem was effectively resolved and what else needs to be done. Reflection, looking back at the original problem or goal to see if it was solved or met, is the final step. Even if the goal was not met, the student's efforts are acknowledged.

During large group time, students are taught how to use these steps. The teacher may use picture cues on a poster, but the purpose is to teach self-management, self-control, self-restructuring, and self-monitoring. Students may be asked to talk through the steps out loud. Eventually they can whisper or use silent talk, pointing to the visualized steps. Students may complete the process by giving themselves positive reinforcement through self-praise, positive self-statements, and other rewards.

Example of problem solving with a behavioral issue:

John and Sara are arguing over a pencil.

"It's mine."

"Is not. It's mine."

Teacher: What's the problem? *(Identify the problem.)*

John: She is trying to take my pencil.

Sara: He won't give me my pencil. It's mine.

Teacher: So *the problem is* that you both want that pencil?

Students: Yes.

Teacher: (Points to goals set by class) What are our goals?.

John: To show respect and responsibility.

Teacher: How could you solve this showing respect and responsibility?
(Generate alternative solutions.)

John: Sara could give it to me nicely.

Sara: John could give it to me nicely.

Teacher: What else could you do?

John: Let her have it. I've got another one.

Sara: I could borrow one from someone else.

Teacher: You have come up with four solutions. Which one will show the best character? *(Evaluate solutions.)*

John: I'll get out another one.

Teacher: Is that okay with you, Sara?

Sara: Yes.

Teacher: Good problem solving. *(Make decision and act upon it.)*

Next time when you both want the same pencil, what will you do?

Often a problem that arose the day before is brought up at morning meeting, and students are guided through the problem-solving process as a group. Here is the kind of dialogue that might occur in a large group problem solving session:

Identify the Problem

Teacher: I noticed yesterday that the art area seemed to be very noisy. It was hard to hear in the rest of the room. Did anyone else notice this problem?

Student: Yes.

Set Goal

Teacher: What is our goal in this class? (She points to list of character traits)

Student: To show respect for others.

Teacher: We all want to respect each other.

Generate Alternative Solutions

Teacher: What could you do about this problem with the noise? How could you solve it in a way that respects everyone?

Mary: Don't let them use boxes.

Teacher: That is one solution. What else could you do?

John: Keep those people out who were in there yesterday.

Teacher: That is another idea. What else?

Robert: We could build something smaller.

Teacher: How small?

Robert: Up to here.

Teacher: So far you have three solutions: 1) Close the art area; 2) Keep the people out who were there yesterday; and 3) Build something smaller. Does anyone have another idea?

Mary: Let them in until it gets noisy and then close it.

Teacher: We have four solutions (She lists them again.)

Evaluate the alternatives

Teacher: Let's look at the first idea. Close the art area. Would everyone be happy with this solution?

Students: No.

Teacher: What about the next suggestion, to keep out the people who were there yesterday. Would you all be happy with that idea?

Students: No.

Teacher: What about setting a rule of making structures only so big. What would happen if we did that? Would it solve the problem?

Students: Yes.

Teacher: So that is one solution we may want to decide on.

Teacher: How about allowing people in there and sending them out if it gets noisy?

Mary: Let's do two things. Allow building only so high and send them out if it is too noisy.

Teacher: Does everyone agree on that solution?

Students: Yes

Plan

Teacher: So we are going to allow the same number of students, but they will only build things this high, and if they get noisy, we will close the center. Who is going in there now?

Evaluate

(At the end of work time, there is another large group time.)

Teacher: How did the art area go today? Did you think it was too loud?

Mary: No, it was okay.

Teacher: Art area people, did you follow your new rule about smaller structures?

Richard: Yes.

Teacher: How did that work?

Robert: Okay.

Peer Mediation

Social problems are those in which students have conflicts with each other. Using problem solving techniques, they are encouraged to talk and listen to the viewpoints of others. They learn to state how they feel and become aware of the feelings of others. They also learn to negotiate (Smith, 1993; Wichert, 1989; Phi Alpha Delta Public Service Center, 1994; Purtzman, Stern, Burger & Godenhamer, 1988; Levin, 1994; Drew, 1987; Bodine, Crawford & Schrumpf, 1994).

Peer mediation uses problem solving and effective listening techniques. A peer mediator does not solve the problems of peers, take sides or judge who is right or wrong, but uses effective listening, and facilitates the problem-solving process. Students volunteer to be mediators, and opposing parties agree to mediation.

The peer mediator uses a mediation form. The mediation meeting begins by reviewing the rules: "The following are not allowed: name calling, blaming, sneering, not listening, getting even, bringing up past problems, threats, pushing, hitting, put downs, bossing, making excuses, not taking responsibility, and interrupting. Do you agree to this?" Both parties must say, "Yes." The mediator then turns to one person and says, "What is the problem?" Students must focus on the problem, not on the other person. The mediator summarizes what the first person said and writes it on the form. Then the second person states the problem from his or her point of view. The mediator recaps what each said and writes it down. Both parties work to clarify what the problem is. The mediator then says, "What is our goal? What character traits are we working on?" and "What can we do about it?" Each party generates solutions, evaluates the solutions, and works at finding a mutually agreeable plan, which is written as a contract that both parties sign (Schmidt, Friedman, & Marvel, 1992).

Helpful Hints for Problem Solving

- When students suggest different kinds of physical violence, the teacher says, "Hitting, kicking, punching, and biting are all sort of alike. What *else* could you do that would be *different*?"
- The teacher can bring others in to help solve the problem. ("Pedro, can you help here? John has a problem.") A third student can be asked to come over and help. Sometimes a class meeting is called on the spot and everyone works together on the problem.
- When a student has used physical aggression, the teacher should be victim oriented, taking care of the student who was hurt, then talking to the aggressive student, helping him or her find better solutions. Many physically aggressive students do not have the functional language to express themselves. The teacher helps them to verbalize and learn meaningful vocabulary, as well as seek out alternative behaviors that better meet their goals and show good character.
- Don't try to determine who started it. Focus on what you can do to fix it or make it right. Encourage negotiation so both win. It is very rare that one student is totally in the right and another totally wrong. When this happens, it is an opportunity for teaching the aggressor how to use better strategies and the victim to use appropriate strategies to protect him or herself.

- When students have employed good problem-solving skills, the teacher should make positive comments about it:
- If no solutions are generated by the students, the teacher may offer choices. Say "I thought of two things you could do. You could ___ or ___. Which would you like to do?" One teacher tells students on the playground that they have to stay next to her until they have thought of solutions. Occasionally, I have suggested solutions I knew the students would not like so that they would want to think of better ones.
- Model problem solving with your own adult problems. Talk out loud using the problem-solving strategies.
- Pictures and cue cards can be posted in the room and on desks to remind everyone of the steps.
- Students who walk aimlessly around the classroom or run around and do not enter into a learning activity are first asked, "What is your plan? What did you plan to do?" If the student says, "I don't know" or continues to move around, the teacher needs to give limited choices: "You may either go to the book area or your desk. Which is it?"
- When students are emotionally upset over a problem, they will not be able to use problem-solving strategies. They need a chance to cool off, calm down, and vent their feelings (see Anger Control). Problem solving is a cognitive exercise and should be done in a calm atmosphere.

Thinking Time

If the student does not follow through on the plan and commitment he or she agreed to, the teacher sends the student to a place in the room away from peers to think, reflect, and plan. The teacher says, "You did not follow your plan, did you? You need to come up with a new plan." When the student has come up with a new plan that is acceptable to the teacher, he or she can join the class. The teacher is supportive and does not give up, even when a student has failed (Glasser, 1993).

If the misbehavior continues, the student is sent to the school disciplinarian and/or a referral is made to the special education coordinator for a more complete analysis. Some students who are unable to manage their own behavior need special classes in behavioral skills. The goal of these classes is to teach character development and behavior management so the student can return to the regular classroom.

Stage Six: Universal Ethical Principles

Stage six thinkers have an internalized belief in universal values. The virtues and ideals described in chapter 3 have become internalized and govern a person's individual morality. This is the goal of character education.

Anger Control: When Cognitive Strategies Don't Work

Kohlberg and Piaget were cognitive psychologists who studied moral reasoning. When people feel very strong emotions, especially anger, they seem incapable of reasoning.

In fact, many misbehaviors in the classroom are inappropriate displays of emotion. Emotions are not morally wrong, but can be displayed through wrongful behavior.

There are times when children (and adults) lose control of themselves because emotions such as anger, frustration or sadness block rational thinking. Everyone needs to release emotional energy regularly. Students need to be shown appropriate ways to express their emotions. Some can write their feelings in a journal, others draw or paint. Many jog or walk as a way of blowing off steam. Sports is a medium for expressing feelings. Some people use dance or drama, others musical instruments. Most often people just talk. Teachers can model appropriate ways to show anger, disappointment, and irritation.

The emotion that causes the most problems in school is anger, because it is often expressed through physical aggression. (Depression and suicide, according to Freud, are self-directed anger.) When a student has lost control, a cool down time or place is needed out of the public eye.

There are relaxation exercises which can be used. LaMaze studied them in Russia and brought them back to France to be used at childbirth. However, they can be used in any stressful situations. Deep breathing, breathing into a paper bag, counting between breaths, relaxing one's muscles, thinking of something pleasant, and other exercises can be practiced for anger reduction.

Relaxation Exercises

Deep Breathing

Take a deep breath, hold it a second, and let it out slowly. Then rest. Inhale, stop, exhale. rest.

Tighten/Tense

Choose the muscles that are the most tense and first tighten them, then relax them. Do this to one muscle at a time. Left fist: tense, relax. Right fist: tense, relax. Wrists, jaw, tongue, lips, chest, shoulder, leg, stomach, neck, biceps, and hips.

Ross Campbell, in his book *How to really love your teenager* (1981), writes about the stages of anger control. The following is a simplification of his ladder.

Phase 1: Passive Aggression

Passive aggression means showing compliance, but with underlying hostility; the appearance of compliance but anger shows in other forms at other times. The children I have worked with who were passive aggressive tended to appear compliant. But they would bite others when I wasn't watching, leave work undone, or not do it at all. A student might sit quietly, but pinch someone when the teacher isn't looking. Incomplete work and not following directions may be indications of passive aggressive anger. Following directions to the letter, but doing so in a way that disturbs others could be an indication of passive aggressive anger. "I'll do what you tell me to, but you'll be sorry" is the thought behind it. According to Campbell, this is the most difficult form of anger to deal with because the student does not honestly and openly confront the issue causing anger. The student may seem to be "in denial" about being angry.

Phase 2: Physical Aggression

Students who hurt others physically, destroy property, or throw objects are physically aggressive. This kind of behavior is dangerous to teachers and students. Anger is shown through violence. Aggression has been categorized as hostile (toward people) and instrumental (toward objects).

Phase 3: Verbal Aggression

At this level students use loud, unpleasant cursing and verbal abuse of others. Anger is shown through yelling, screaming, cursing and name-calling.

Phase 4: Verbal Release

At this level normal voice tone is used, but unrelated complaints are included. Anger is displaced to other sources and people, so it is hard to get at the root cause. There is a lack of focus; many problems are all brought up together in an irrational manner. One complaint after another is tossed onto a mounting pile that seems to defy solutions. Many of us are at this level.

Phase 5: Positive Problem Solving

Here we hold to the primary complaint, think logically, focus on the source of the problem; seek resolution and are pleasant about it.

Use of Levels

I have found Campbell's levels helpful in dealing with anger. Dealing with violence (Phases 2 and 3) requires specialized training in physical restraint. Every school should have an emergency plan, and teachers should be prepared to use it. After the cool down period, when the student is calm, Campbell states that adults should affirm children's anger. The teacher should compliment the student for the positive aspects of anger shown and then encourage the student to move to the next phase. For example, when a student has hit or hurt someone, the teacher should say, "You showed that you are angry (it's better than being passive aggressive). You need to use your words." The teacher might model words which could be used and have the student practice.

When a student screams and yells, the teacher responds, "Using words to express your anger is good. Please use a quieter voice." When a child uses a Phase 4 expression of anger, the teacher says, "I'm pleased that you are able to talk about this in a calm manner. Let's stick to the issues and figure out how to resolve them." Anger needs to be affirmed and accepted, or it will be channeled into self-destructive behavior such as alcohol, drugs, suicide, running away, vandalism, and sexual acting out. There are many harmful and life-threatening ways that anger is expressed.

Social Dysfunction

Some behavior problems are a product of the social milieu of the classroom. Behavior problems due to social conditions should not always be construed as character flaws. When student groups become noisy and rowdy, the number in each group can be reduced. The teacher merely says, "Three to a group" or "Two to a group." If the problem persists, it is "Back to your seats." Another technique is to say, "Form a group with people you have not worked with before." Dr. Hal Urban has high school students sit next to someone different every day. Seat placement and re-arranging membership in a group are time-honored techniques teachers use to eliminate misbehavior.

Whenever people are together, social skills are needed. Some students are lacking in social competence. This means they are unable to read a social situation and act appropriately. They most often invade the space of others by touching peers who do not like it, interrupting conversations, speaking loudly, disrupting other social interactions in progress, and ruining the work of others. They do not read and react appropriately to nonverbal signals. For example, other students may frown, edge away, tense up, or turn away. Instead of adjusting by showing behavior that gains approval, they persist in their negative behavior until they are verbally rejected. When others reject and insult them, they mirror the behavior back by doing the same, creating a downward spiral of social incompetence and rejection. These students are usually picked on and used as scapegoats for the whole class. They are at risk of dropping out of school, becoming runaways, and joining a negative subculture such as a gang or group using drugs, alcohol, or prostitution.

Students who are constantly behaving negatively and are rejected by the class need intensive therapy in recognizing non-verbal signals and correcting their behavior. They can learn to give appropriate compliments, to have a skill or talent that others value, and to enter a social situation appropriately and end it gracefully. There are programs like the Responsive Classroom, which specifically addresses the social curriculum.

Socially incompetent students need a calm place with more space, a designated place to stay, and fewer interactions with others, because they are overstimulated and overwhelmed with normal classroom interactions. They are usually rejected in small groups using cooperative learning, but can do well at paired learning.

Class size can have an effect on character development. In large classes and classes with very needy children, it is difficult to address individual moral needs. In smaller classes, there is more attention to individual needs and growth.

Multiaged classes tend to show more altruistic behavior as older children help younger. There is more cooperation and less competition. Another advantage of the multiaged class is that students have the same teacher for more than one year. The stronger the teacher/student relationship, the greater the potential for character development.

Summary

Even when classroom governance has been established democratically and well, behavior problems will arise. Misbehavior is at least to some degree a reflection of the student's character and provides an opportunity for character education. Because students have not yet formed habits of behavior, the teacher cues them both nonverbally and verbally. Eye contact, gestures, facial expressions, touch, proximity and signals are nonverbal cues. Reminders, hints, questions, challenges and "I messages" are verbal but nondirective cues.

When students have done something wrong, the teacher begins the correction process by listening to what the student has to say. The teacher uses questions to help students solve their own behavior problems. Using Kohlberg's stages of moral reasoning helps us understand how children think, their view of right and wrong. Teachers have used punishment, rewards, praise, consequences, problem solving, and character education.

Uncontrolled emotions have caused violence and many other destructive behaviors. Teachers can find ways for students to express their anger appropriately.

Sometimes behavior problems are a product of the social curriculum and disappear through social skills training and rearrangement of the environment, schedule, class size, and multiaged classes.

Exercises for Teachers

1. *Describe problems students frequently have and how you handle it. For example, two students fight over something or students are not following the rules.*
2. *Use the checklist in the Appendix for assessing problem solving in your classroom.*
3. *Examine your own style of discipline. Which stage does it most closely resemble (punishment, reward, approval, rules and consequences, problem solving, or appealing to universal values)?*
4. *How do you went your anger? What healthy outlets do students have?*

CHAPTER 7

Character Education Through The Curriculum

Curriculum refers to the subject matter being taught and the approach used. Character education is taught both through **content** and **process** (Tomlinson & Quinton, 1986). For example, students in an art class may learn about moral values by studying statues and memorials. Here character education is being addressed through subject matter or content. Character education may also be taught by having students work together on a mural about clouds. The process of working together builds character, even though the topic is not necessarily moral in nature.

There are four different ways that character education is being taught through the curriculum:

1) As a separate subject called character education, moral education or ethics;

2) Integrated thematically through webbing a character trait;

3) Infused within the regular curriculum by using a lens which brings moral issues into focus;

4) Informally.

A Separate Subject

Some teachers have chosen to set aside a block of time for teaching values and moral education weekly. Michael Schulman, in his book *School as moral community* (1995), recommends that students take a class or course in moral reasoning called "Ethics" or "Character Education." The classroom teacher or specialist sets aside anywhere between thirty and ninety minutes a week taking one, two, or three sessions to focus on moral issues. There are published curricula such as that of the Character Education Institute, which has a kit for each grade. The kit has a teacher's manual with lessons and activities, worksheets for students, posters, and materials. It can be used as a "stand alone" program, but is also a jumping off point for including character education in everything that happens in the classroom.

Sample Lesson from Character Education Institute

Objective: At the conclusion of these lessons, your students should be able to give examples of honest and dishonest behavior at home and at school.

Step 1: Read the following story to the children:

What Should Melissa Do?

One day Melissa's mother sent her to the store to buy a loaf of bread. She gave Melissa a dollar and told her to bring back the change. At the store Melissa found the kind of bread her mother used and took it to the check-out counter. She gave the dollar to the clerk. The clerk thought it was a five dollar bill and gave Melissa more change than she should have. Melissa's first thought was, "Great, now I can keep this money. After all, it's the clerk's mistake, not mine." Then she thought, "Would that be the honest thing to do?" Melissa knew she had been given too much money. She had to decide whether she ought to keep the money or return it. Many thoughts came to her. "What should I do?" she asked herself.

Step 2: Divide the children into small groups and have each group develop an ending for the story. Ask them to share their ending with the rest of the class by telling or role-playing the decision and the results.

Step 3: Discuss the consequences of the decisions presented by the groups. Elicit from the students that it would be wrong not to return the money to the clerk.

An Integrated Approach

Some teachers use a thematic approach to curriculum because it more closely matches how the brain acquires information. In a thematic approach, learning is not divided into subject areas such as reading, mathematics, science, and social studies. A topic or book is the central focus of the curriculum, and all learning is related to that central theme. The curriculum is designed as a web, emanating from the center.

A character trait is central to the curriculum. Here is a sample outline of a year's curriculum using the integrated, thematic approach:

September	Friendship
October	Kindness
November	Hard Work
December	Giving
January	Respect
February	Honesty
March	Responsibility
April	Respect for environment
May	Citizenship

Sometimes a book becomes the central focus. The Heartwood Institute has developed a web using a book. The following is an introductory sample of a thematic unit based on the character trait of friendship:

Friendship Unit

Goal: *Students will know what friendship is. Students will learn the skills of making and keeping friends. Students will value friendship. Students will form friendships with each other within the class.*

Students will befriend people outside the classroom: younger children or older people.

Books: *My friend, Obadiah, Ira sleeps over*

Stories and Fables: *Damon and Pythias, Antigone and the lion, Hamlet and Brutus, Cyrano de Bergerac*

Songs: *"It's a small world after all"*

  "I'd like to teach the world to sing"

  "Make new friends but keep the old. One is silver and the other gold."

  "The more we get together, together, together. The more we get together, the happier we'll be. For your friends are my friends, and my friends are your friends. The more we get together, the happier we'll be."

  Have students make up songs about friendship.

Discussion: *What is a friend?*

  How do you choose a friend?

  How do you make a friend?

  How could you lose a friend?

  What makes friendship last?

  How do you know if someone is a true friend?

  What virtues or character qualities do you need to keep a friendship strong?

Pledge: *Write a pledge on friendship for the class.*

Flag: *Design a friendship flag.*

Art: *Use the rainbow as a symbol of friendship.*

  Make posters about friends.

  Make a friendship mural as a class.

Mottos: *A true friend walks in when the rest of the world walks out.*

  Friendship is like a bank account. You can't continue to draw on it without making deposits.

  The only way to have a friend is to be one.

Creative Movement: *Dance with a friend. Circle dances as a class.*

Drama: *Role play issues around friendship: How to form a friendship.*

How to start a conversation. How to offer or ask for assistance. How to deal with a conflict over what to do together, sharing resources, differences of opinions.

Use puppets to role play ways to form friendships.

Games: *Have students play board games together.*

Use commercially prepared games such as the Friendship Game.

Videos about Friendship: *Barney videos; Mr. Roger's Neighborhood*

Math: *Create word problems about friends.*

Have students work together to solve problems.

Discuss how friends help each other without intruding.

Have students work on math projects together: measuring object in the school, etc.

Science: *Discuss the meaning of symbiosis and parasites. Describe life forms which are both. What is the difference? Discuss how these two concepts can be seen in human relationships.*

Social Studies: *Discuss famous friendships in the period of history being studied. Discuss the effect of bad friendships in current events and history.*

Multicultural: *Find out how people show friendship in different cultures. While friendship is valued around the world, each culture has its own way of showing it.*

Outdoor: *Extend outdoor time beyond a 15-minute recess, and teach students games such as Mexican Hide Out, a variation of Hide and Go Seek where they join the person hiding.*

Celebrations: *Have a Friends Day similar to a party. All activities that day are meant to build friendship. Sometimes students can invite a friend from another class or school.*

Language Arts: *Students write poems, essays, and short stories about friendship.*

Bulletin Board: *Make a bulletin board with the title: Our Class Friends. Have each student's picture on it.*

Special Needs: *Discuss how to be a friend to someone with a handicap-*

ping condition. Ask a student with a disability to talk about what is and is not appropriate.

Unit on Heroes

One teacher used the central theme of heroes and heroines. She first talked about the difference between heroes and celebrities, and the kinds of traits that make someone a hero. Celebrities are made famous by the media. They make news, but not necessarily history. Heroes are known for achievements, portraying ideals, and making a difference in the lives of others. They may not be great in the eyes of everyone, but they have a powerful impact on the life of the person who sees them as a hero. The class then studied heroes and heroines from history: authors, characters in books and movies, historical figures, mathematicians, scientists, artists, musicians, and sports figures. The teacher chose people from the historical period designated for that grade level, as well as people who matched ethnicity, socioeconomic background, gender, interests, and disabilities of students in the class. Students looked for heroic traits as they read and researched. Portraits and posters depicting these heroes and heroines were hung on the walls. Students read biographies and autobiographies of good people.

Community members

Students studied living heroes. There are heroes throughout the local community who can be brought to the classroom or interviewed. Students interview them to learn about their heroic acts and their values. They may be older people, a successful business person, grandparents, parents, or government officials. The historical society may be able to furnish community heroes and heroines. Foster grandparent programs, veteran organizations, and nursing homes are good places for finding living heroes. *Reader's Digest* and local newspapers often feature these citizen heroes. Our local newspaper publisher has a dinner once a year to honor people who have performed heroic acts that year. The Giraffe Project (see References) honors those who "stick their neck out" for others. Sometimes heroes and heroines are bus drivers, cafeteria workers, and custodians who have done something extraordinary. When they are portrayed as people worthy of admiration, students treat them with more respect.

We all, young and old, learn much from example. Most of us follow people even more than ideas. We do what those whom we admire do. Personages from Jesus to Albert Schweitzer to Mother Teresa to Martin Luther King Jr. have symbolized that truism, and, as the Nazis showed the world, there are other kinds of models to follow (Morality, 1992).

Student Heroes and Heroines

Finally, students themselves work to become like their heroes and heroines through community service. According to Kilpatrick (1992) each person has an innate desire to be a hero or heroine of his or her own life. When we try to act the way we want our heroes and heroines to act, this brings out the highest qualities of character.

One class of third graders at Memorial School in Bedford, New Hampshire, was given a writing assignment to describe their heroes or heroines and tell why that person was chosen. Here is a sample of their responses (with the original spelling and grammar):

My hero is my mom. She has brown eyes. She is very pretty and nice. The reason why I picked my mom is because she brings me places like soccer and gymnastics. That's my hero. Alyssa, age 9

My hero is Jack Humphrey. Jack was the first person to train Dogs to help the Blind. He was also the one to think it up. His first dog he trained was Buddy who was owned by Mr. Frank. I admire his ability to train both dogs and Humans. He has brought dogs and Humans closer together. Breana, age 9

My hero is Sally Ride, the first American women and the youngest astronaut ever to orbit the earth. She was the subject of my biography book talk. She is a very smart person, who earned a doctoral degree in astrophysics. She is a very courageous person and I want to be like her! I admire Sally Ride because she did something no American woman had done before. She studied and worked hard to go into space. She always had a positive attitude about everything that she did. She is a true worker, who would never give up on anything. Joclyn, 9

My heroes or the people who I think of as heroes are the people in the wars. They fought for our country. The people in wars saved many lives. One of the qualities that the people in the wars have is that they were brave. The people in the wars were smart, slick and fast. The people in the wars gave their lives for our country. That is why the people in the wars are heroes to me. Adam age 9

The Person I admire is... My kindergarten teacher because she died of cancer. We, (everyone) that was in her class made a quilt for her. The 1994 class made a film strip about her. They're making a Patty's Place on the playground. For the playground at the town pool there's going to be a brick with her name on it. I really miss her. Katie Age 9

Sharon Banas in Sweet Home, New York, has her students write star poems about their heroes. The poem has the following construction:

two qualities

verb

sentence about hero's qualities and/or accomplishments

These poems can be copied on yellow paper, cut in the shape of a star, and taped to the ceiling.

Some teachers have students write a letter to the hero or heroine of their choice and see if that person will come to the school or write back. Students can research a hero of their choosing and prepare a presentation, playing the part of the hero through drama. They can apply what they learned about the hero by asking, "If *(hero)* were here, how might he/she go about dealing with *(a problem in student lives, school, or community)*? For example, "If Martin Luther King were here, how might he deal with school violence?" Students can find famous sayings by their hero or heroine. These can be written, memorized, and recited.

Teachers who have taught a unit on heroes and heroines have found that their students better understand the concept of character. It has been said, "Tell me your hero and I will tell you your value system." Perhaps the best way to develop good values in our students is to provide them with good models. While this has been a time-honored form of character education, we have to address the fact that all human beings, including cultural heroes and heroines, have faults, failings, and character flaws, some more glaring or heinous than others. Teachers used to glorify the good and ignore the bad in our country's heroes. They also emphasized the bad and ignored the good in villains like Benedict Arnold. This kind of "black and white" thinking especially appeals to young children. I remember thinking everyone in the world was either good or bad. I would ask my mother, "Is that a good guy or a bad guy?" I'm not sure how well young children can understand that good adults have done bad things, and vice versa.

A major tragedy of the OJ Simpson case was the fact that he was a hero to so many African-American boys. His athletic and acting successes were admirable. The shock came in finding out that he was not thoroughly good in all aspects of his life. At the third White House conference on character education Hillary Clinton was asked, "How can we have heroes and heroines among politicians, when there is so much scandal?" Her answer was that we should focus on the character qualities being exemplified, rather than the person.

Infused into the Curriculum

Most teachers feel they do not have enough hours in the school day to add another subject, called an "add on." Character education can be infused into the established curriculum by looking for the moral issues that naturally arise in the subject matter. For example, a study of the American Revolution could include discussing civil disobedience, the moral framework of the United States Constitution, and the moral principles they were fighting for. A study of *Johnny Tremain* would include looking at the moral aspects of the book: What should Johnny do? Who had done right? Who had done wrong? Some teachers, such as those in Stratham, New Hampshire, have spent staff meetings going over their curriculum and highlighting the moral issues. How can the curriculum be mined for its moral content? Those using this approach say character education and good curriculum are synonymous, meaning that if a curriculum in any subject is truly quality, character education is included. Literature, language arts, social studies, science, math, computers, vocational education, music, art, modern language, family and consumer, science, guidance, health, physical education are all subjects in which character education can be taught.

The following sections show how each subject in the curriculum can be a springboard for character education.

Stories and Literature

For thousands of years the universal method of moral education was storytelling. The story is a basic and powerful form which has been used in all cultures to teach about right and wrong (Egan, 1986). Stories pass on the great tradition, our cultural heritage. Every good story has moral value (Coles, 1989). Teachers help students discover and discuss those values and look for personal application in their own lives (Wanner, 1994; Parr, 1982). The characters in stories become remembered voices that invade and influence the conscience. One high school English teacher who took a workshop with me said she grew up in a dysfunctional family lacking in morals. The characters in stories gave her the moral fabric her home life lacked.

The oldest form of moral literature is the parable, and anecdotes are the most common form of moral instruction. Stories with moral messages have also been conveyed through myths, ballads, statues, paintings, film, and videos.

Holidays are times for learning about the character of famous people: Martin Luther King Day, Abraham Lincoln's birthday, George Washington's birthday, Women's History Month, Black History Month, etc. Biographies provide curriculum for character education.

There are at least four different literature-based character education curricula. The Heartwood Curriculum has chosen seven virtues and offers a series of grade-level books. There is a teacher's guide for each book. Young People's Press has published books such as *Stories of fairness* and *Stories of kindness*. Many of the stories are reprints of great pieces of literature by Oscar Wilde and Brothers Grimm, as well as stories from other cultures. The Center for Learning is especially helpful for middle and high school teachers who wish to infuse character education in their literature curriculum. It publishes teacher guides for a wide range of novels, plays, and commonly taught books. The Developmental Studies Center in California also uses literature and has published guides for teaching specific books in elementary school. *The loving well curriculum* (Boston University, 1993) is a fascinating anthology of short stories about intimacy designed for middle school. *The Book of virtues* (1993) and *The Moral compass* (1995), edited by William Bennett, are two anthologies every teacher should have. *The Book of virtues* is organized by character trait. *A call to character* (1995), edited by Colin Greer and Herbert Kohl, is another anthology which contains excellent character-building stories.

Bibliotherapy is used to help people deal with difficulties. By reading about others who faced similar situations, students take courage to press on. *Book finder* (Dreyer, 1994) is a reference book that lists moral and social concerns, as well as storybooks or trade books in which those concerns are addressed. There are several annotated bibliographies for character education: *Books that build character* (Kilpatrick, 1994), *Why Johnny can't tell right from wrong* (Kilpatrick, 1992), *Honey for a child's heart* (Hung, 1989), and *Books children love* (Wilson, 1987).

Students at every age like to be read to. Historically, stories were meant to be **heard**. Story telling and being read to develop auditory skills, as well as good listening habits. I read a picture book at each of my college classes. Because picture books are short, they are easy to include in a seventy-five minute class. Older students can become "book buddies" and read to younger students as a form of service learning. Students can take books home and read to their parents. This is one form of parent involvement. Parents can also be encouraged to read to their children.

My colleague Dr. Marna Bunce-Crim had each college student choose a picture book and write learning activities based on the book. The materials needed to complete the activities were put in a decorated box, along with a copy of the book and an audio tape of the book read out loud. The kit was sent home, and parents were asked to use it and write a note to the college student evaluating it. This type of homework helped parents become involved in their child's learning.

Shared reading (students reading together in unison) of poetry, pledges, songs, chants, mottos, and big books brings a sense of community and togetherness. Students who are not yet reading well can follow along.

Paired reading, where students take turns reading to a partner, teaches the skills of taking turns, contributing, listening, supporting, and evaluating.

Language Arts

Language arts is an opportunity for students to use the spoken and written word to develop their own character. Morning meetings and class meetings are often used for encouraging verbal expression. The teacher might throw out a question for all to answer. A typical sharing session might begin with one of the following questions:

- *Tell us how you got your name.*
- *What is something you are very proud of?*
- *If you could teach everybody in the world just one thing, what would it be?*
- *If you were the president, what would you do to make the world a better place?*

Students might be asked to complete a sentence. The teacher writes the first part of the sentence on newsprint or the chalk board. Each student finishes the sentence out loud. Sometimes responses are recorded. Here are some sentence starters:

- *When I get angry I should...*
- *I felt brave when...*

- *When I make a mistake I...*
- *I want to be admired for being...*
- *I'm getting better at...*
- *I helped...*
- *People seem to respect me when I...*
- *I made a good decision when I...*
- *The things I look for in a friend are...*
- *I like people who...*
- *I believe...*
- *I am a good friend because ...*

Sometimes the following games are used at a class meeting:

1. Guessing Game— The teacher begins by describing a character trait shown by someone in the room. Students guess which classmate it is. The person who guesses correctly gets to describe the character trait and good deed of someone else in the room.

2. Choose one student's name out of a hat. Other students give compliments, describing examples of good character.

3. Feely Bag— Put various objects in a bag. Play music and have students pass the bag. When the music stops, the person holding the bag takes something out and gives a brief object lesson with a moral. Others can help if asked. For example, if the object is a butter knife, the student might say, "Don't try to butter people up. Be sincere."

4. The game *Choices* (three versions: Children's, Teen, Adult) can be used for large group. The teacher chooses a card and reads the situation. Students vote, thumbs up or down for yes or no, then discuss their responses in light of specific character traits. Here is a sample card:

   "In the middle of an important math exam you realize that your best friend is copying your answers. Your teacher has said that anyone caught cheating will be given a zero and taken to the principal. Will you tell?"

5. Students enjoy acting out skits or pantomimes such as "The Turnip" (McCaslin, 1990). Assign roles of grandfather, grandmother, and

granddaughter before you start the story. Then point to other students to join as you go along. The teacher may decide to play the part of grandfather.

The Turnip

A Russian folktale. All the class can take part.

It was autumn and time for the turnips to be harvested. Grandfather went out to the garden and bent down to pull the first one. But this turnip was different from any turnips he had ever planted. It refused to come up! So, after trying unsuccessfully with all his might, he called his wife to help him. When grandmother came out and saw what he wanted, she got behind him and put her arms around his waist, and together they pulled and pulled. Still the turnip would not budge. Then granddaughter came out to the garden to see what was happening. Putting her arms around grandmother's waist, she pulled grandmother, who pulled grandfather, who pulled the turnip. But the turnip refused to come up.

(Continue until all characters have become included, each pulling the one before him. Sometimes the granddaughter's dog pulls her and a beetle pulls the dog, followed by a second, third, and fourth beetle.)

Finally, when all pull together, the turnip comes up!

6. Here are other pantomimes which your students may enjoy. In a **pantomime,** no words are spoken. Students use body language or mime to convey what is happening.

a. **Patience** *(Two people— a bus driver and a passenger).* You are going on a field trip to which you have looked forward for a long time. *(Pause for action.)* You get in the bus but the bus will not start. *(Pause for action.)* After a few minutes, the driver lets you know that he cannot make it go, and so your trip must be postponed. *(Pause for action.)* Disappointed, you get out. *(Pause for action.)* Suddenly, the engine starts. *(Pause for action.)* You turn around and see the driver motioning for you to get back in. Your happiness is great because you can now go after all.

b. **Kindness** *(Three or more people — guest, friend, mother, etc.).*

You are invited to dinner at the home of your friend. You help yourself liberally to the potato salad, which you like very much *(Pause for action.)*, but when you take your first bite, you think something is wrong with it. *(Pause for action.)* Should you go on eating or leave a large serving on your plate? Should you say something to your hostess? You look around the table. What are the others doing?

7. **Improvisation**— In an improvisation, there is no script but words are spoken. The actors think up the words as they go along.

Improvisation 1: You are in the middle of a reading group when you look up and notice your favorite souvenir from vacation is no longer on your desk. Who took it? What do you do about it? Is it found? Each student shows a reaction to this situation.

Improvisation 2: A new student has entered your class at school and does not speak English. Some of the students laugh at him/her. When recess comes, you all go out to the playground. How do each of you treat the newcomer? Do you include or exclude him/her?

Improvisation 3: You and your friend find a five dollar bill on the playground. You want to keep it, but at this moment another student comes looking for something. You are certain she has lost it. What do you do?

Improvisation 4: You see the girl across the aisle cheat on a test when the teacher steps out of the room. The teacher suspects there has been cheating and asks you and the girl to stay after class to find out about it. What do you each say and do?

Writing Assignments

Students are usually asked to write on a daily basis. Often teachers have the writing assignments posted so that students begin the day writing while attendance and other administrative details are being taken care of. Students can keep "ethics journals" describing the moral choices they have made. Here are other suggestions for journal writing assignments:

1. Write about a special event in your life. How did it affect your character?

2. Make a personal time line showing significant events that have affected your character development.

3. Write an acrostic using one of the universal values. Here is an example:

H	Hear ye, hear ye
O	Only honesty works
N	Never take something that doesn't belong to you
E	Even if you want to
S	Show sincerity
T	Tell the truth
Y	You will be glad you did

4. Write a poem using the virtue. Give guidelines for the type of poem (haiku, etc.).

   Courtesy

   Some people are rude

   And others are crude

   But, if you care

   And want to share

   Then practice courtesy every day

   And all rewards will come your way!

5. Students can be asked to divide one page in their journal into four equally-sized boxes. In the first box they write, "Where am I?" In the next box, "Where am I going?" In the third, "What obstacles do I face?" and in the fourth, "What inner quality will I need to overcome these obstacles?" Students answer each question.

6. Imagine that you have been given a time machine and are on your death bed. What do you want people to say about you? What virtues do you want to have showed? What motto do you want your life to have exemplified?

7. Like *Pilgrim's progress*, each person's life can be mapped out. Make a story map of your life. Parents could be asked to help with this by providing dates.

8. Choose one virtue such as honesty or love. Use colored markers to

write the word in any kind of lettering you choose. Make a design around the word.

9. Choose a virtue and write it at the top of the page. Then write as many examples as you can. For example, "Honesty is..."

10. When you have a tough decision to make, what do you do? List strategies.

Sometimes everyone contributes one page to a class book. For example, the book might be titled "We are courageous." Each student uses one page to write a story about showing courage.

Handwriting

Handwriting used to be taken very seriously before the days of computer technology because it was said to reveal character. Students were taught the need for clarity and consistency through penmanship drills.

The teachers who still teach handwriting may use mottos and famous sayings for handwriting practice.

Letter writing has been used for advocacy campaigns, letters to the editor of the local newspaper, and Amnesty International. Amnesty International is an organization that works to free political prisoners through letter-writing campaigns. The United States Postal Service has designed a school program called "Wee Deliver." Students write letters to each other and mail them. This fosters handwriting practice, as well as communication and friendship.

Spelling and Vocabulary

What does a person's spelling reveal about character? What character trait is associated with misspelled words? In the past, poor spelling was associated with sloppiness, inaccuracy, laziness, and indifference. Perhaps this is even more true with computer software to check spelling available!

Some teachers give weekly spelling and vocabulary lists for students to memorize. They may begin with making a spelling list of names of students in the class (first and/or last names). As students learn to spell each others' names correctly, they are building a sense of community. Teachers have also used character traits for one to three of the spelling or vocabulary words on the list. For example, students might learn about prudence one week and temperance another week.

Social Studies

Some people think social studies is the subject which best lends itself to character education. When I looked through college notes for the fourteen methods courses I took (!) in the 1970s, Methods of Teaching Social Studies had a section on values education. History, civics, current events, and the study of other cultures are included in social studies. These subjects contain many moral issues.

The purpose of public education is to prepare citizens for democracy. Civic education is a priority of education, and citizenship is often listed as an important character trait. Patriotism is a debated character trait because it has been misused. However, students need to develop a sense of identity, belonging, and pride in their country. There are excellent programs for teaching civic education such as that of the Center for Civic Education, which has developed recommended assessment frameworks in civics for grades 4 through 12. The best way to begin is through the kind of self-governance described in chapter 6.

If we are to participate in the global arena, we need to understand other cultures. Social studies teachers have found many interesting ways to teach about other countries. I remember doing a contract on a specific country back in the 1950s. Now teachers work with travel agents who provide posters, video tapes, and travel brochures. Students have pen pals and e-mail, using the worldwide web. They send environmental exchange boxes so that students in another country receive artifacts of our culture and send artifacts of theirs. Students cook ethnic foods, wear native costumes and jewelry, read authentic literature, listen to music, learn dances, and play games. They study the values of other cultures. How are those values demonstrated? How are they like ours?

How are they different? At its best, the study of other cultures builds understanding, empathy, respect, and tolerance.

The following are some activities for teaching character education through social studies:

Government/Civics Education

1. Study the founding documents of our country for the virtues they espoused: the U.S. Constitution, the Mayflower Compact, the Bill of Rights, and the Declaration of Independence. Memorize the Bill of Rights. Study the state constitution and state laws. Visit the state legislature to learn about how laws are made. Visit the state Supreme Court.

2. Study the laws and legal system in order to better understand the concept of justice. The law-related education committee of the American Bar Association has developed projects such as mock trial competitions, a "Lawyer in Every Classroom Day," and materials about character education.

   a. Hold a courtroom drama where students role play a case.

   b. Describe juvenile law: the boundaries, responsibilities, protection and penalties for young people. Police officers and lawyers are usually willing to come into the classroom to explain laws to students. *Everyday law for young citizens* (Lipson & Lipson, 1988) is an excellent resource for participatory learning about law.

   c. Study Supreme Court decisions.

3. Study the moral philosophies of different forms of government such as communism, socialism, and capitalism.

4. Study community helpers: people who are contributing to the community's welfare. For example, you might study school board members, selectmen, volunteer fire fighters, the United Way, the Lion's Club, and the Rotary Club (see chapter 8).

History

1. Use holidays to study our cultural heritage and the values we esteem. *Child Craft Encyclopedia* has a comprehensive yearly calendar with anniversaries and holidays. Civil Rights Day, Presidents' Day, Veterans Day, Memorial Day, and Thanksgiving are each meant to celebrate specific virtues.

2. Study the speeches of famous Americans. Presidential addresses, such as the Gettysburg Address, often cover ethical issues. Analyze, paraphrase, summarize, and memorize these.

3. Identify moral themes and dilemmas throughout history: prejudice and intolerance versus civil rights; treatment of ethnic groups, such as Native Americans, Jews, Catholics, Japanese during World War II; war and peace; greed versus giving; power and control versus freedom; attitudes toward slavery; the family and its changing role.

   A middle school in Weare, New Hampshire, has combined literature and social studies into one subject, and students spend one term studying a moral concept through history and literature. For example, they may study war and peace for one term. They read such novels as *All quiet on the western front* and study about wars in history. In another term, they study about intolerance and civil rights. "Facing History and Ourselves" and "Teaching Tolerance" are programs for looking at racial inequities.

4. Use local history, living people, and family members to personalize modern history. Provide role models of moral courage.

5. Role play and dramatize periods of history, such as the pioneer days or life at a medieval castle. What character qualities did people of those times display? What virtues were most valued? How were they displayed? Compare lifestyles then and now. What character traits did they have to show? Do we need the same traits? Do we show them differently?

6. Use movies like *Glory* and *Fat man and little boy*, which portray moral issues in history. *Glory* is the story of an African-American

regiment during the Civil War. *Fat man and Little boy* describes the decisions made about the atomic bomb in World War II.

Geography

1. Study the interaction between people and geography. Have humans used or misused their world? How do the environment and people sometimes come into conflict? How do they work together?
2. Use maps to learn about how geography influences one's value systems. *National Geographic* magazine has a geography contest, encouraging students to learn about other parts of the world.

Current Events

Analyze newspaper articles for moral issues. Once I started looking for articles, I found one almost daily. Use articles to discuss world and national problems and how to solve them. Have students use the newspaper to write their own moral dilemmas. This requires that they analyze newspaper and magazine articles for the moral issues raised. For example, "There are so many deer in Conway County, they are dying of starvation. Would you provide incentives for deer hunting? Why or why not?"

Science

How do science and character education go together? When Aristotle introduced science, it was so that humans could assume the role of caretakers and stewards of the natural world. Historically, scientists have viewed themselves as preserving and enhancing the world for the betterment of the human race. Science is approached with respect for all life, concern for endangered species, a desire to protect and preserve habitats, and a true appreciation for our natural environment. Biology is based on respect for life. As students watch an egg hatch, they can experience the wonder of life. Respect for the earth's resources includes reusing, recycling, and reducing the amount of waste.

Character traits such as objectivity, accuracy, precision, pursuit of truth, problem solving, intellectual and academic honesty, courage, humility, logic, integrity, diligence, persistence, curiosity, and imagination are most often mentioned in connection with science. Students can learn about objectivity through hypothesis testing and the scientific method, being honest in reporting data, even when data does not support the hypothesis.

The New Hampshire Curriculum Frameworks (1995) state that the purpose of science education is "to sustain, maintain and improve the quality of life on earth for the future, to enhance democratic societies and the global economy. The goal of science education is not only to produce scientists, but also to prepare well rounded, clear thinking, scientifically-literate citizens. To help young people acquire the knowledge, skills (and values) they will need as productive adults in an increasingly technological society is the major purpose for science instruction."

Many science experiments are conducted through cooperative learning. Students learn to work together and share responsibility for the outcome. They practice taking turns and respecting the views of others. They can discuss the inter-connectedness and interdependence of the planet, studying topics like global warming, rain forests, and water cycles, which are nature's examples of cooperation.

Responsibility for science equipment is very important. Students can learn to keep themselves safe by taking responsibility for the equipment they use.

The following are activities for integrating science and character education:

1. Discuss ethical issues in science on topics such as genetic engineering, experiments on people and animals, and disagreements between businesses and scientists in the tobacco and asbestos industries. Students can read newspaper articles about medical research, environmental legislation and governmental regulation, nuclear energy and other scientific issues. They can discuss the moral aspect of these controversies. "Survival of the fittest" and survival in nature

have moral implications which can be explored. Students can discuss the risks in science such as space research (the Challenger) and medical experiments.

2. Study famous scientists and "the story behind science." Many scientists, like Louis Pasteur, were great humanitarians.

3. Take responsibility for a service project to beautify the environment. For example, in one elementary school they decided to beautify a part of the playground. Students planted shrubs and flowers.

4. Celebrate Earth Day through projects, artwork, dramatization, decorations, and speeches.

5. Take care of class plants, pets, or a bird feeder outside the window.

6. Build and protect habitats for birds and animals.

7. Plant a tree on Arbor Day.

Math

Mathematics calls for scrupulous honesty, meticulous accuracy, and integrity. For example, what if a decimal point is missing or in the wrong place? What if a zero is missing? What can be the consequences when computation is incorrect at the store or bank, or when laying carpet, measuring lumber, or cooking?

There are many situations in which numbers have been handled inaccurately— for instance, when one has been given too much or too little change at the grocery store, when one has been overcharged for an item, and when one has reported incorrectly on his/her tax returns. The moral aspects of marking up prices, writing "rubber checks," paying people "under the table," manipulating statistics to project false conclusions, foreclosing due to high interest rates, fraud, embezzlement, robbery, false bankruptcy and insurance claims, and stock market schemes all involve math.

Teachers have identified specific virtues needed in math: honesty, accuracy, courage, compassion and helpfulness toward each other, persistence and diligence. Cooperative learning has been found to reduce "math phobia."

Here are some specific exercises that combine math and character education:

1. Compose word problems in which universal values are incorporated.
2. Study famous mathematicians. Many were humanitarians.
3. Students can conduct surveys on moral issues and learn to record the results accurately. For example, "Would you cheat on a test if you knew you would not get caught?" "Have you cheated within the past term?"
4. Students can keep frequency counts of "good deeds" and do statistical analyses using graphs. For example, the frequency of the following traits can be tabulated: kindness, patience, peaceful conflict resolution, courage, honesty, and fairness.
5. Students can learn life skills like balancing a checkbook (accuracy) or budgeting for shopping (prudence). Give students exercises in which they have to make wise economic choices using a menu, catalogue, or grocery flyer. The introduction of coupons can help in understanding real numbers, as well as in developing frugality.
6. Set up situations in which students can demonstrate honesty and responsibility with money: a class store, a fund-raiser, or a class business.

Computers

Computer technology opens up a vast expanse of information. Plagiarism, pirating, and copying software have become easy. The ethics of technology use is extremely important.

The word processor can be used to create stories which have moral themes. It can be used for calligraphy and graphics. The use of the internet and other software in the area of character education is in its beginning stages.

Vocational Education

In New Hampshire, a business in education task force composed of members of the business community identified the skills needed in the work force, so that schools could prepare competent future workers (1991). That list included: courtesy; respect for human worth and property; respect for human diversity; responsibility to oneself, to one's family, to others and to the community; a regard for commitments and obligations, fulfillment of one's citizenship obligations; preparedness, an awareness of the environment; dependability and honesty; fairness; regard for law, right action, constitutional rights and democratic principles as applied to individuals; self-respect, self-control, and a sense of personal worth; and recognition of choice and personal discipline.

One small business owner spoke up in one of my workshops and said, "I hire and fire people based on their character. It is rarely a lack of intelligence, but poor work habits that cause people to get fired. If they have the character traits of punctuality, dependability, honesty, a willingness to work, and cooperation, I can teach them the job skills needed. If they don't have these character traits, I'm wasting my time and money training them."

Here are some approaches used by vocational teachers regarding character education:

1. Students make a list of ethical issues in the workplace: What makes a good employee or employer?

2. Study the ethical issues in each career. For example, "What kind of character is needed for a good doctor, teacher, business executive, etc.? What moral issues do they face?"

3. Involve students in community learning. Collaborate with businesses by taking students to job sites and bringing employers to school. Have guest speakers tell stories about when they need to show character.

4. Have the class or groups of students choose a project through which they help a nonprofit business. They might paint a mural on a day-care center wall, paint a hall of a rest home, or clean up trash at a vacant lot.

5. Start a recycling business for aluminum cans, glass, paper, or cloth.

6. Discuss the proper care of equipment and the consequences of

carefulness, as well as carelessness. One businessman described a tragedy in a third world country wherein a disgruntled employee of a *Fortune* 500 company turned on a valve and released deadly gasses into the community. The head of the company flew to the site and said, "I assume full moral responsibility for this." He spent millions of company dollars to rectify the problem. What kind of character did this show?

Music

Music is a vehicle for expressing cherished values. Songs, marches, operas, operettas, musicals, and many other musical forms have stirred the moral passions of people throughout history. Music reflects the culture and its values. Teachers have used music such as anthems to provide a common culture and sense of togetherness, as well as to stir students to depths of feeling. Music can be emotionally powerful as a moral force.

Character education can be taught through studying specific musical works (content) or by writing and using music (process). When students learn vocal and breath control, this is a form of self-control. Singing or playing as a group teaches cooperation and teamwork.

The following are a few activities in which music has been used to teach character education.

1. Students write a song promoting universal values. They often use a familiar tune. Here is a song composed at one workshop:

> *Respect*
> *(Sing to "Twinkle, Twinkle, Little Star")*
> *Respect each other every day*
> *In what you do and what you say.*
> *Show each other that you care.*
> *When they need help you're always there.*
> *Respect each other every day,*
> *In what you do and what you say.*

2. Study ballads and songs for the character traits or flaws portrayed. Learn about the composer and why the music came into being.

3. Discuss the moral issues around "stickered" music and how music has been used to promote negative values. Discuss the qualities of good music.

4. Discuss the moral issues around slavery and sing Negro spirituals.

5. Study music as it related to values in each period of history and culture.

6. Watch movies such as *Mr. Holland's Opus* and *Immortal Beloved* (the story of Beethoven) for their moral content.

Art

Art conveys the values of the culture. Monuments, memorials, sculptures, and paintings have promoted the enduring value of beauty. Students can learn to appreciate and respect visual beauty in many forms (Wezeman, 1990). They can also learn to use the visual arts as a form of self-expression.

There are many art forms students can use to promote good character.

1. Draw a picture that illustrates one of the universal values. Draw pictures of good and bad behavior.

2. Design a poster or banner about a character trait.

3. A collage can be used to illustrate "Who am I?" and "What virtues do I cherish?"

4. Talk about colors and the character traits they symbolize. For example, blue represents loyalty.

5. Make a peace necklace or other form of symbolic jewelry.

6. Design cards for holidays, using uplifting messages.

Modern Language

Language describes culture. Through studying language, students learn about a culture, its values, and its unique words and ways of expressing virtue. Students learn to accept, respect, and admire other cultures.

1. Songs, dances, games, holidays, literature, artifacts, and customs from other cultures can demonstrate or illustrate values.
2. Have students greet each other in a different language and learn culturally appropriate ways of showing friendship.
3. Have students make friends with people from other cultures through pen pals, exchange students, or e-mail.

Family and Consumer Science

Shirley Ochs at Lebanon Junior High School in New Hampshire is a home economics teacher who teaches a unit on interpersonal relations. It includes acceptance of physical, emotional, cultural, and intellectual differences; improving communication with family and peers; discipline versus punishment; and dealing with peer pressure. She uses open forums. Her classes also work in groups, in which they grapple with issues such as nonparticipants, making group choices, and accepting individual responsibility within a group. An important skill she teaches is decision making: making informed decisions, collecting information, and understanding the consequences.

Guidance

Guidance in elementary school includes teaching social skills, behavior management, affective education (the study of feelings), and crisis management. In guidance classes, students can learn about how to get along with others, make and keep friends, resolve conflicts, use self-control, express emotions appropriately, and handle crises. They can learn peaceful ways to settle differences. Some guidance counselors go into regular classrooms as specialists and teach a guidance class once a week. They may use commercial programs such as the DUSO kit (*Developing Understanding of Self and Others*), *Social Problem Solving Curriculum* by Spivack and Shure, games such as *The Self Control Game*, or activities from books such as William Kreidler's *Creative conflict resolution* (1984). They may teach peer mediation, peaceful conflict resolution, and anger management. Guidance counselors often do a unit on abuse: how to prevent it, how to identify it, and what to do when abuse has occurred. They may teach about "stranger danger" and how to keep oneself safe. Sometimes guidance counselors teach health: good health practices and sex education.

Here are some typical character-building exercises used by guidance counselors:

1. Describe a situation in which you were upset:

   Situation   Feelings   Character Trait Needed

2. Play a game. The teacher says, "Use your face to show a feeling and we will guess what the feeling is. Use your arms and face to show a feeling. Everyone will guess what the feeling is. How else could you show that feeling?" Teach students how to display feelings appropriately, using body language and words.

3. If you had a problem, whom could you talk to? Whom do you trust? Make a list of people.

Health

Respect and responsibility for self and others is the foundation of health education. The focus of alcohol, drug, and sex education units should be respect and responsibility for self and others. Good nutrition and wellness are promoting respect for our bodies.

There are sex education programs based on character education. The premise is that sexual behavior has a moral aspect. Tom Lickona has said that the most important moral decisions adolescents make are those regarding sexual behavior. He has written articles and taught many workshops on sex education and character education.

Physical Education

The primary goal of a physical education program is teaching lifelong care of one's physical body through exercise. This is why health and physical education have been taught as one subject. Healthy lifestyles are the focus of physical education. A second aspect of physical education is teaching how to participate in team sports. Virtues such as fair play, teamwork, cooperation, and respect for others are part of good sportsmanship.

There are national sports leagues that are making statements about the need for character. At the second White House conference on character education, one board member of the American Youth Soccer Association said, "When our sports programs cease to become character building programs, they have lost their reason for existence." A task force of the Communitarian Network has developed a position statement regarding sports and character education.

Several authors, such as Russ Geough (1996) and Jim Thompson (1995), have written about sports and character education. Jeff Beedy has developed a Sports Plus program (1996), and Joseph Bowab has written and piloted a literature-based sports program that can be used by the regular classroom teacher or in after-school programs.

Bette Frazier, a physical education teacher at Carpenter School in Wolfeboro, New Hampshire, was given a "Book of Compliments" for Christmas by a fifth grade class. Each child had decorated a file card and written a personal note about her teaching and why the class enjoyed their physical education class.

Bette gives a small, construction paper heart-shaped love note to each kindergarten student after physical education classes. On the note is a message to their parents such as, "Please take a walk with me," "Let's bounce a ball," or "Ask me about muscles."

Here are some character-building activities involving sports.

1. Examine codes of ethics for sports (see Josephson Institute Code of Ethics for Sports). Discuss common situations and how to handle them ethically:

   a. The referee calls a bad play.

   b. An opposing team member breaks a rule but is not caught.

   c. Your team is losing and you could bring your team's score up by hogging the ball.

    d. A fellow team member makes a ghastly error. What do you do?

    e. When your team wins, how do you treat opposing players?

    f. When your team loses, how do you treat opposing players?

    g. You could tell the coach about another team member who did something wrong.

2. Discuss the ethical issues around competitiveness: "It's not whether you win or lose, its how you play the game," "Try your best," and the value of competing with oneself. Discuss "fair play." What is it? Why use it? What is "unfair play"?

3. Play sports in which students must encourage each other in order to stay in the game. Players who are the most encouraging get to keep playing. If they stop encouraging others, they have to sit out. Students on the bench must encourage others in order to get back in the game. This is called "Satterfied Ball," named after Peter Satterfield, a sixth grade teacher.

4. One teacher used stations in the gym. Each station featured a piece of equipment or physical exercise. Students were expected to stay at one station until the music stopped. Then they were to give someone a compliment and move on to the next station.

5. Having teams shake hands before and after a game is one way of teaching respect.

6. Biographies and movies of famous athletes provide rich material for discussing issues of character. *Chariots of Fire* is filled with moral decisions and courage.

7. As students collect baseball cards and cards from other sports, they can learn about the good things these athletes have done. Unfortunately, a great deal of publicity has been given to the moral mistakes of a few athletes. Even they can provide fodder for moral discussion.

Informal Curriculum

Informal teaching means maximizing the situations that arise in daily classroom life. Students may come in from recess and want to talk about a situation that arose. There may be an argument during cooperative learning. An area of the classroom may be very messy. The teacher uses the naturally occurring experiences to "seize the moment" for teaching about character. Life's experiences are training in character education. These become the "teachable moment," because interest and involvement are high.

A skillful teacher will engineer the teachable moment by providing time and opportunities for students to make choices and decisions, interact with each other, and work together. Through experiences, difficulties will arise. They become opportunities for learning.

The teacher may ask questions to help students think clearly about values. Sometimes the teacher takes a neutral stance and asks the student to think about consequences and values. Using a Socratic approach, the teacher asks, "What will happen if you do that?" "What would be the right thing to do?" and "What character trait should you be showing?" Questions are used to challenge incorrect assumptions.

Another approach is to build empathy by asking students to identify the feelings of others. When students are upset, they are coached to use words to describe their feelings. This helps others become more aware, and the more students can identify the feelings of others, the more empathic they will be. Most teachers will say they have always taught character education. They are referring to this informal method. I believe the informal curriculum is not enough of itself, that students need a more planned, thought-out, and pro-active curriculum which includes direct instruction *before* anything happens. There needs to be an established framework which gives meaning to experience.

Once this has been provided by the teacher, the informal curriculum provides examples from everyday life.

Summary

Character education is taught through curriculum in four ways: as a separate course; integrated thematically around a virtue, book, or topic such as heroes; infused in the regular curriculum; and informally through the teachable moment. There are advantages to each of the above and to using a combination of all of them. Most teachers choose to infuse the regular curriculum.

Exercises

1. *Use a copy of your curriculum guide or frameworks to decide what virtues you will emphasize through content.*
2. *Use a highlighter in your lesson plan book to show where character education will be emphasized.*
3. *Make a list of character traits to be taught with each unit of study.*
4. *Make a chart for each subject you will teach.*

   Math

   Skill: Addition

   Character trait: accuracy, persistence

   Reading

   Book: Johnny Tremain

   Character traits: tolerance, empathy, honesty

CHAPTER 8

Class Projects

COMMUNITY SERVICE LEARNING

A class project is any undertaking in which students work together for a good cause. The project might be putting on a play, producing a newspaper, organizing a fund-raiser, community service learning or planning an advocacy campaign.

Individual Responsibilities

Students of good character take responsibility for themselves as individuals by keeping their desks neat, hanging up coats and hats, being economical with paper and pencils, turning in completed assignments on time, and producing quality work.

Classroom Responsibilities

Students can reach out beyond their individual responsibilities by caring for others and sharing responsibility within the classroom. Many teachers have a system of class helpers who perform various tasks or classroom chores. They may hold the flag, turn on the lights, open and close the windows, take messages to the office, be line leaders, take care of equipment, water the plants, feed the pets, keep the classroom clean, help the substitute teacher, and greet visitors. These chores are usually rotated weekly or monthly.

Sharon Huot, a third grade teacher in Bedford, New Hampshire, has her students fill out applications for classroom jobs. They also have to submit a letter of recommendation (usually filled out by their mothers). She has found this to be a good way for them to learn about the world of work. It also means that the most qualified (or usually interested) student gets the job and produces quality work— or else gets fired.

Another type of activity for teaching classroom responsibility is a class project. A "friendship quilt" is a class project in which each student decorates a square, and the squares are sewn together to form a quilt. It may be used as a school decoration, raffled off for a fund-raiser, or donated to a needy family. Students might work together on a class mural which decorates one wall of the classroom or hall. They plan together regarding the theme and assign space to each class member. The teacher might make a large floor puzzle out of tagboard (or wood that is cut with a jig saw), giving each student one piece to decorate in a way that describes what he or she contributes to the class. It is then placed at the game center. The teacher might use a large piece of newsprint and divide it into squares, one square for each class member. Students write their names in the squares and draw symbols for their expertise and talents, which can be shared with the class. There might be a Who's Who or Who Can Do It chart, on which each person's strengths are listed so that students can access each other as resources. The class might publish a book in which each student contributes a short story, poem, drawing, or recipe. It is always interesting to read the recipes kindergarten students write (or dictate) for their favorite family dish.

Some classes produce a newspaper. Let's examine how a class newspaper promotes character. Students must assign roles: who will write, who will print, and who will distribute the newspaper. Jobs such as illustration and layout must be divided fairly. A newspaper can be the place to air and share ideas and concerns about moral issues. Students can write their opinions through letters to the editor, editorials, and opposing editorials. Public opinion surveys can be conducted. No obscenity, name calling or rumor mongering are allowed. Students use cooperation, teamwork, responsibility, respect, and good citizenship.

School Projects

The class can reach out beyond the classroom and choose a project to make the school a better place. This kind of project encourages students to care about something in the school outside the classroom. The project could be keeping one hallway clean and decorated, planting bulbs around the outside of the building, taking care of a bathroom or section of the cafeteria. They might begin a school-wide recycling project or fund-raiser.

Other types of projects within the school are book buddies (where an older class reads to a younger class), tutoring, mentoring, peer mediation, and safety patrol. At the Villa Augustina School in Goffstown, New Hampshire, the eighth graders read to the kindergarten children once a week. Helping younger children increases their ability to care for others. Being a tutor has great educational benefit. "I never really learned it until I had to teach it" is a common remark made by tutors. Many schools have instituted peer mediation programs through which students learn mediation skills and become designated peer mediators. A safety patrol program trains older students to take responsibility for younger children on the bus or in the cafeteria. Safety patrol officers may wear a uniform, carry a badge, or have some other form of designation.

These are a few of the many possibilities for projects within the school. The class may take a tour of the building and grounds on the first day of school and choose a project based on what they see. Sometimes the principal has a list of possibilities from which to choose. Often each class is assigned certain tasks such as a hall bulletin board.

Reaching out beyond the classroom into the shared spaces of the school builds a sense of caring, teamwork, and community.

Community Projects

There are three kinds of community projects which will be discussed here: social science research, community service learning and advocacy.

Social Science Research

Students may be given an assignment to collect information (called *data*) in the community. They could mail a survey, conduct telephone interviews, meet people in person, audio or videotape their interviews, and take photographs or draw pictures of where they went and whom they met.

Whenever students are sent out into the community, the teacher should write a cover letter explaining the exact nature of the assignment. The teacher has a responsibility to consider potential misinterpretations and misuses of the research, and should make every effort to communicate results so that misunderstanding is minimized.

Here are ethical guidelines for this kind of research. They are adapted from the code of ethics of the American Psychological Association (Cozby, Worden, & Kee, 1989; Mcmillan & Schumacker, 1984). The term **subjects** refers to the people in the community being contacted. The term **investigator** refers to students.

The teacher is responsible for the ethical standards. The teacher and student(s) should inform the subjects of all aspects of the research that might influence their willingness to participate. They should be as open and honest with the subjects as possible. All subjects have the option to refuse to participate, with no adverse consequences. Subjects must be protected from physical and mental discomfort, harm, and danger.

Most studies require the investigators to secure informed consent from the subjects before they participate in the research. This means the subjects agree to participate, based on full disclosure of what the research is about and any risks involved. Subjects can terminate their participation at any time with no penalty. Subjects should never be coerced into participating. Some research, which clearly has no risks to the participants and is conducted unobtrusively (in which individuals are unaware that they are subjects, as in the use of town reports or community statistics), needs no informed consent.

Information obtained about the subjects must be kept confidential unless disclosure is otherwise agreed upon in advance through informed consent. Often, in order to protect the anonymity of the subjects, only group data is reported.

Examples of Social Science Research

History. Research genealogies and countries of ancestry; the history of various landmarks in the vicinity of the school: houses, geographical landmarks, industries, government buildings, and school buildings; famous people and their descendants; older people.

Ask questions such as:

What was your first car?

How did you feel about it?

What was your first job?

How much did you make?

What did you learn from the experience?

What values did your parents teach you?

How were you taught morals in school? Describe a time when you were honest or dishonest, when you showed courage or bravery, when you were kind or unkind.

How should children show respect? How have you had to take responsibility?

Current Events. Talk to people who are in the news or who do something newsworthy. Ask them about their value system.

Religion. Interview communicants or clergy of different faiths. Ask about their value systems.

Art. Visit museums, buildings with noteworthy architecture, statues, monuments, and showings in public buildings. What value is being portrayed?

Music. Talk with musicians in bands and orchestras. Ask about the values being portrayed in their music.

Math. Ask people how they use math every day. How are they honest or dishonest in their use of numbers?

Science. Ask people how they use science in their homes and in their jobs. How do they show respect for natural resources? How do they protect and preserve the environment? How do they promote plant and animal life?

Students may collect information from the community for written reports, graphs, charts, maps, outlines, time lines, auditory reports on cassette tapes, oral and videotaped reports. The information may be used for writing poetry, plays, newspaper accounts, editorials, or essays. Students may draw or paint pictures, posters, or illustrated texts.

The community contains a wealth of resource information which can become a valuable part of the curriculum.

Here is a sample letter that a teacher might send with students who plan to conduct research in the community:

Dear _____:

*(Student's name)*_____ is a student at Clark School in Amherst, NH, and I am his/her teacher. The students are visiting veterans of World War II. Would you be willing to talk about your experiences? The student will ask you a few questions. You do not have to answer every question. If, for any reason, you are uncomfortable answering a question, just say so. The student will be writing a report and using your name. If you would like a copy of the report, please give the student your name and address.

If you have questions or suggestions, please feel free to call me between 8:00 and 8:30 A.M. at 673-1122.

Thank you for your help.

Sincerely yours,

Mary Smith

Grade 3 teacher

Here is a sample informed consent form:

I,_____(name of community par-
ticipant), agree to participate in this research project about
_____(topic of research). I would like to see
the final project. (If so, write name, address and telephone
number.)

_____

Here is a sample parental consent form (used when their child will
be interviewed or tested):

I give permission for my child_____(name
of child) to participate in this project _____
_____(name of project).

Parent signature:_____Date:_____

Learn and Serve

Historically, an important character trait was charity. "Those who
have" felt a moral obligation to help "those who have not." Philan-
thropic giving has been a hallmark of good character. The classroom
teacher looks for ways to encourage student generosity toward the less
fortunate through donations of material goods and service. Voluntary
service is called **volunteerism**. Some schools and social agencies which
actively promote volunteerism and improvement of the community
have made it mandatory. When it is not voluntary, it is called **community service**. Community service has both a moral and a civic purpose.
Morally, students learn to give to their communities, to serve others.
The civic purpose is to help maintain the community and participate in
community life. Students can learn more from community service when
it is treated as a learning experience and is supervised by educators.
This is called **community service learning**. Community service learn-

ing is rooted in moral, civic and vocational education, in philanthropy, volunteerism, community service and field work. It has a moral aspect (*charity and philanthropy*), a civic aspect (*citizenship, community involvement, and taking responsibility for our world*), and an educational aspect (*field-based learning*) (Zlotkowski, 1995). It is an intentional, planned exchange of learning and benefit— a combination of educating students and meeting community needs. The teacher chooses experiences which connect the content of the curriculum to the challenges that exist in the community. Both the curriculum and the community are enhanced, as well as the professional development of the student. Learning objectives are based on both the curriculum and community needs. Service and learning are combined through the moral principle of servant leadership.

Vocational Education. The history of vocational education goes back to the Middle Ages when there was a system wherein students served an apprenticeship to a master workman. Many occupations have a field work component called **community learning.** Most pre-professional programs at the high school and college level grant academic credit for practicum, internships, and field work. These experiences are utilitarian, emphasizing work-related skills. They can be enhanced when they are also providing a community service.

Educational Benefits. Students practice their newly learned skills and understanding through active participation in community life. They connect theory to practice through experiential learning. They engage in active learning, finding out about different careers and taking a leadership role. Students build relationships and a sense of community by being part of a team, working together in partnership with others, and taking part in the human family. They also benefit from intergenerational learning and spending time with people in the community who are more experienced. It is educationally sound because students are engaged in authentic, meaningful, useful experiences.

Community Benefit. The community receives free labor and other resources. Meaningful projects are sustained. Students bring new life, creative ideas and energy, as well as current trends and knowledge learned in their courses. Teachers often serve in a consultative role both for community organizations and students.

Moral Benefit. Community service learning is morally valuable because students use their moral imaginations and impulse toward idealism, coupled with academic rigor, to promote a moral ideal. Their work is morally significant. They have direct experience with a community's need and organizations that promote public good. Students look at their own values and responses to larger societal questions.

Examples of Community Service Learning Opportunities

English. Work in the town or city library by putting away books, reading to children in the children's section, helping the reference librarian, or performing any task that involves books and reading.

Spend time at a newspaper office watching how articles are written and edited; going with a reporter and writing up an article, and then comparing it with the article written by the reporter.

Volunteer at a television or radio station by watching how they put news together, practicing reading the news, helping to write copy such as public service announcements, and watching the editing process.

Serve as a tutor for immigrants learning English; serve in a literacy program for adults; help younger children in an after-school program with their homework.

Math. Shadow a banker; learn how money is counted and books are kept; learn some of the skills of a bank teller.

Spend time in an accounting department or with a bookkeeper in order to learn how figures are kept.

Learn how to use a cash register, accept payment, and count change; keep track of the money collected in a fund-raiser; work with the cashier in the cafeteria.

Serve as a math tutor for younger students in an after-school program.

Science. Visit a pharmacy and watch how the pharmacist measures and weighs out prescriptions; learn the skills of measuring and weighing.

Visit a manufacturing firm such as a paper company where chemists are mixing chemicals; learn about the change process.

Spend time with a game warden, engineer, meteorologist, or at the town dump; see how each of these uses science to improve our world and quality of life.

Social Studies. Spend time at a historical society, museum, public works (geography) department, town or state government office, lawyer's office, court, political campaign headquarters, legislature, town meeting, or police department.

Students may be sent in groups of two or three, or as a class. They may go to a site during class time or have it assigned as homework. There might be a "career day" where they shadow a professional. For example, students interested in becoming teachers can work in a school or child care center. Those who want to go into health care can spend time at a hospital or doctor's office. Every area of business is a potential site for community service learning. The community is rich in possibilities. Some schools have developed partnerships with a particular company or organization and have developed continuous collaborations. The school-to-work initiative bridges the gap between education and community businesses.

Students of all ages should be participating in community service learning. The youngest children can sponsor a needy child through Save the Children; make cards and draw pictures for people in nursing homes; or donate old toys, stuffed animals, books and outgrown clothes to other less fortunate children. Older children may help younger children in their own school, another school, or a child care center. They may stock a soup kitchen or recycle empty soda cans or paper. They may collect canned goods, clothes, or blankets for the needy.

Robin Grumman, a teacher at Unity School, takes her middle school students to a nursing home, which is within walking distance of the school. The students visit the elderly one afternoon a week. In her curriculum she discusses the aging process, how our society treats the elderly, and what the elderly have to offer the community. By respecting, tolerating and befriending the elderly, these students are developing character. One year, a patient they were visiting died. She included learning about death in the curriculum. The students attended the funeral and gave a eulogy.

Community service learning requires the same kind of supervision as other kinds of learning. The teacher prepares the students for the experience by talking about it ahead of time and emphasizing the ethical requirements. The teacher contacts the community organization and provides the information it needs, observes the students on site where appropriate, reads their journals, and discusses the experience with them.

Students process their experience through writing journals and reflection papers, class discussions, small group sharing sessions, and individual conferences with the teacher. There is usually a final evaluation by student, teacher and the site supervisor, called the cooperating teacher.

I recommend the following sequence for community learning:

Phase 1: Observation. This is an extremely important skill. Being able to closely observe what an expert is doing takes concentration. If students are going to use imitative learning, they have to have observation skills. Being able to observe is an important life skill that is too often neglected.

Phase 2: Helper. The student is an extra pair of hands—a "gopher" (go for this and go for that)— and helps as needed.

Phase 3: Pre-professional. The student engages in mini-assignments or projects which require preparation on the student's part. The student writes out a plan which must be approved by the cooperating teacher. The cooperating teacher observes and evaluates the student in action.

Phase 4: Leadership. The student actually assumes a professional position, at the same level as the cooperating teacher. The cooperating teacher serves as observer and evaluator.

Advocacy

Advocacy combines social science research and community service learning. Students identify a moral issue within the discipline they are studying, and use their newly acquired knowledge or skill as a moral force for good. They systematically work on a project for the good of the community, to "make the world a better place." They may use letter-writing skills to write letters for a worthy cause. They may adopt a highway, raise funds for a worthy cause, or build a picnic table.

Here is a guide for implementing an advocacy campaign in the classroom:

Planning

Students choose an area of interest within the curriculum. For example, recycling, substance abuse, care for the elderly, nuclear waste, second-hand smoke, or child abuse.

Academic Research

They go to the library to find books, articles, published and internet information in order to gain more knowledge about the topic.

Social Science Research

Students collect information from people in the community by making telephone calls to local organizations dealing with the topic. They read brochures and fact sheets developed by these organizations. They learn about their own community's needs. *Kids count* and *150 ways teens can make a difference* (Salzman & Reisgies, 1991) are books which offer telephone numbers and mailing addresses of organizations.

Community Service Learning

Students plan and implement an activity. For example, they might start a recycling project by collecting cans, newspapers, or bottles. They may stock a soup kitchen, write letters to impact legislation, build a community playground, or work on a campaign. Students can become involved with local government by addressing the mayor, board of selectmen, or city council about their concerns. They may bring media attention to the issue.

Reflection

Active participation should be followed by debriefing and opportunities for further involvement. Students reflect on their experience, what they learned, and how their beliefs and attitudes have changed. They draw conclusions and find challenges for future work. This component reinforces knowledge and curriculum content. The reflection is recorded either by:

- keeping a journal or writing an essay, poem, or letter;
- designing a poster, display, brochure, fact sheet, or documentary;
- an oral presentation such as serving on a panel, being videotaped, giving a talk, or participating in a discussion or debate.

Community Service and Volunteer Work

Community service, wherein students do a project which is unrelated to academic work, and volunteerism, wherein students offer to do unpaid work that is not assigned or required, are best addressed through cocurricular activities after school. Many schools have a service club, which is primarily student-run, with the help of an adult advisor. Latchkey children can take part in community service rather than sit at home in front of the television. Community service may be the best antidote to loneliness.

Some schools have a specified number of hours of community service as a graduation requirement, but if students have not been adequately mentored through their community service assignment, it can be counterproductive. For example, students sent to a nursing home could come away with an aversion to the elderly, and thinking we should just kill them to save society money! There must be preparation, careful monitoring, and follow up. Students need to process what they see, hear, and do. They need guided discussion and help to look beyond the disagreeable.

Harmin (1990) believes that everyone has an inner desire to help others in need, to contribute to our world, to be involved and needed, to do something meaningful, and to have a sense of accomplishment. Young people need to feel that something or someone depends on them, that without them the world would be deficient. They want to make an impact on their world.

He writes to young people:

> You are important to the world. You are needed. Most of all, you can make a difference in someone else's life. Begin by doing something that shows you care. That's where satisfaction in life begins. And if one day, you get a feeling that says you can change the world, trust that feeling. Because you can make a difference. There is something important that needs to happen in the world because of you, and it can happen if you do it. Despite the fact that adolescents are maturing physically at an earlier age, we keep postponing the time when we allow them to contribute to society and test their capacities as adult participants. We are wasting a million kids a year. It's a crime the way we try to stall the process of maturity by holding youth in abeyance (throughout high school and college). Youngsters need to have responsible roles. They need roles that involve decision-making and experiences that develop their caring for others. They need to feel that they can make a difference in the world around them. They must be given opportunities to channel their energies in constructive ways. I believe most young people would choose constructive ways to use their energies if such ways were made available to them. If their impact can't be constructive, it may well be destructive. They need to be noticed and valued, the need to make a difference must be expressed in one way or another.

Principles of Good Practice for Combining Service and Learning

An effective program:

- Engages people in responsible and challenging actions for the common good.
- Is committed to program participation by and with diverse populations.

- Articulates clear service and learning goals for everyone involved.
- Allows for those with needs to define those needs.
- Clarifies the responsibilities of each person and organization involved.
- Matches service providers and service needs.
- Expects genuine, active, and sustained organizational commitment.
- Includes training, supervision, monitoring, support, recognition, and evaluation to meet service and learning goals.
- Insures that the time commitment for service and learning is flexible, appropriate, and in the best interests of all involved.
- Provides structured opportunities for people to reflect critically on their experience.

Resource People in the Classroom

Sometimes students cannot go out into the community, so the teacher brings the community to them through resource people. For example, there is a program called "adopt a grandparent," where retired people come into the classroom to spend time with students. A librarian, police officer, lawyer, banker, store owner and realtor can visit the class and describe the ethical issues in their respective professions. The local pharmacist can show how chemistry pertains to caring for the sick. Doctors can present the humanitarian purpose of biology and life sciences. Surveyors and engineers can discuss the purpose of their jobs in relation to earth and physical sciences and the ethical implications of what they do. Parents can be asked to talk about their jobs: how they use math and the ethical implications of error, the written records they keep, and other ethical issues. Even teachers have to compute grades and turn in attendance records and lunch counts. What happens if they are inaccurate?

Sometimes people can talk about the mistakes they made. One school brought prisoners to talk about the bad choices they made and their regrets. Teen mothers have spoken about the responsibilities of motherhood.

The best visits by resource people include hands-on activities with real life materials, artifacts, pieces of equipment for the students to handle, uniforms to try on, brochures, and things that they use in their work. The teacher may need to prompt guests regarding these things ahead of time. The teacher helps students learn the name and title of the resource person so that he or she can be addressed correctly. Students are taught how to show good manners toward visitors. Students and the teacher ask questions, rather than listen to a lecture. Students may be asked to prepare questions in writing ahead of time. The teacher models the role of learner, asking questions and showing enthusiasm for learning. The teacher might ask, "What would happen if you were dishonest?" "Are any people in your profession dishonest?" "What are some difficult ethical decisions you have had to make?" "How have you had to show courage?" "How have you had to show trustworthiness?" "If someone is going to be successful in your field, what character traits should be shown?"

After the visit, students can discuss, write, or dramatize what they learned. They may write a thank you letter. Pictures can be taken and used for the class history or publicity in the local newspaper. A bulletin board can be devoted to information about the visitor. Students can read books or use the internet to locate more information and prepare a written or oral report.

Summary

Effective class projects begin with and are grounded in the academic program. They bring academia and good character together through use of the moral imagination, promoting ideals, and service. For example, if students are learning how to read, they then help someone else learn to read, or students learn how to cook and then cook for someone else. Students, under the guidance of the teacher can apply classroom knowledge in a way that benefits others.

Exercises

1. *Make a list of classroom chores. Ask students how these could be accomplished.*
2. *Tour the building. Choose an area that the class will work to keep clean. Ask students to make a plan.*
3. *Look through the curriculum and choose a curriculum-based community service learning project.*

CHAPTER 9

Assessment Of Character Education

Assessment of character and character education is an essential part of the teaching process. Character education will only be taken seriously when it is subject to the same level of accountability as other educational programs. Because it involves beliefs, as well as knowledge and behavior, the assessment of character education must be approached in a thoughtful manner. There have been many discussions on the topic of assessment among character educators. Some schools measure the effectiveness of their character education program by looking at the frequency of absenteeism, tardiness, vandalism, and drug use. Tom Lickona has developed an "Eleven Principles Survey (EPS) of Character Education Effectiveness." David Wangaard from the School for Ethical Education has piloted another school-wide instrument. Because this book is about the classroom, this chapter addresses assessment of students, classroom, and classroom teachers. The Character Development Foundation publishes an assessment tool for classroom teachers who wish to measure implementation of the LC5 model in the classroom. Here is a guide for developing your own assessment.

All teachers use informal assessment techniques such as oral and body language, showing approval or disapproval of student behavior. Students assess each other the same way. However, this chapter outlines more structured approaches.

The assessment process begins with **selecting the criteria**. What exactly will be measured? When character traits and goals have been chosen and defined in behavioral terms, (see chapters 1 and 2) they become the criteria for assessment. Students and teacher together may establish these criteria.

The next step is to find or **design an assessment tool or instrument**. It might be a checklist, rating scale, chart, rubric, paper/pencil test (such as true/false, multiple choice, short answer, or essay). It might be a diary, journal, anecdotal record, portfolio, or profile. There are many forms of assessment, and teachers usually design their own.

The final step is to **determine the method** for using the assessment tool. Who will use it? How? When? Where?

Conduct Grades

Traditionally, there was a "conduct" section on report cards, and teachers graded students each term. Under the conduct section were behavior indicators such as "gets along well with others," "follows directions," and "manners," written in the form of a **checklist**. Teachers either checked the areas where a student did well or where a student needed to improve. Sometimes there was a scale of one or two. One meant satisfactory, two meant needs improvement.

Teachers who choose to use this form of assessment will list the universal values which the class chose to work on:

Sample Checklist 1:

Conduct (S= satisfactory; N= needs improvement)

___ Trustworthy	___ Respectful
___ Responsible	___ Fair
___ Caring	___ Citizenship

The teacher may decide to describe specific behaviors listed in the definition of each trait. For example:

Sample Checklist 2:

Trustworthiness:

___ Completes homework

___ Attends classes regularly

___ Follows directions

___ Follows through on commitments

Checklists can be completed quickly and are easy to use. All students are measured on the same behaviors. However, there are disadvantages to checklists. Rater bias (dislike or favoritism), selective memory, and guesswork threaten their accuracy. Ratings are often based on intuition. A checklist does not show how frequently or well the behavior was exhibited, and the student may have shown character traits that are not on the checklist.

Rating Scale

A rating scale is similar to a checklist. In fact, a checklist may be turned into a rating scale. There is a list of identified character traits and a specified scale. The Likert scale (1 — 6: 6 is high, 1 is low) is the most common. A report card is a rating scale using letters instead of numbers. A rating scale is easy to use, code, and analyze. However, one may question how precise it really is. The reason for the rating is not explained. It may also reflect the bias of the person filling it out.

Sample Rating Scale

1=does not exhibit this trait; 2=needs improvement; 3=slightly less than satisfactory; 4=satisfactory; 5=very good; 6=exceptional.

___ Trustworthy

___ Responsible

___ Respectful

___ Fair

___ Caring

Jeff Beedy at New Hampton School in New Hampshire and Barry Kibbel at the University of Oregon have both developed indicators for each number on the rating scale. Beedy's scale is as follows:

1: Student is disruptive, openly defiant, avoids the virtue.

2: Student observes others and does right when "I'm stuck with it."

3: Student shows a clear understanding of the virtue and generally or usually uses it.

4: Student seeks opportunities to use this virtue.

5: Student models for others and helps them show this virtue.

Kibbel's scale (based on the idea that people go from dabbler to novice, to apprentice, to expert, to champion) is as follows:

1: recognizes the character trait in others

2: recognizes the need of it for self

3: tries out the virtue

4: accommodates or internalizes the virtue

5: promotes the virtue

6: seeds the environment

7: guides others

8: personifies it

By defining the numbers, the rating is clarified.

Anecdotal Records

Anecdotal records are usually written by the teacher. However, students and parents could learn how to record them as well. Each entry is dated. Specific incidents are described in narrative form. Following the description is an evaluative summary.

Anecdotal Record Sample

Date: March 5, 1999

Place: Classroom

People involved: John Doe and other students

Summary of incident:

I was delayed at the door by another teacher. The students were at their seats, and the assignments were on the board. While many of the students were wasting time with off task behavior, *John Doe* was quietly working at his seat.

Analysis or Interpretation:

This showed me that John can be trusted to do assigned tasks whether I am watching or not.

Here is an anecdotal record using a fight form:

Summary Written by Student

Who fought? John, Tom and I.

Why did you fight? Tom came over and pushed me, so I pushed him back. Then he pushed me harder. John came over and pushed me too. We pushed harder until the teacher came and separated us.

How did you feel? angry, scared.

What happens next? How can you solve this problem? Walk away? Try to make friends?

What character trait do you need to show? Self-control.

Although the writer is expected to use objective reporting, anecdotal records can be biased and subjective. Writing the entries can be time consuming.

Diary and Journal

The earliest form of assessment was the diary, where adults wrote a summary of the child's behavior at the end of the day. Daily entries described a child's progress. Since it was based on memory, it was not always accurate, and diaries written by parents were found to be lacking in objectivity. A great deal of the collected information might have been irrelevant.

Journals have become popular in the past decade. They are similar to diaries in that there are narrative entries, often written by students themselves. Journals are usually written weekly or twice a week. They often include illustrative drawings. Some teachers have students keep ethics journals. The entries might include moral questions the student is wrestling with and difficult situations the student faces. One problem with using diaries and journals as assessment tools is that students may not be completely honest in what they write. They are forced to disclose information that may incriminate them or others. This diminishes the effectiveness of the journal as an assessment instrument.

Portfolio

Students collect information to document their character development. There may be a section for each virtue, in which students include samples of their work. There might be journal entries, drawings, diagrams, cartoons, an essay, poem, play, or short story the student has written for creative writing or enjoyed reading as literature. It may include a photograph, video, or audio tape. For example, a student may make a poster or mural depicting trustworthiness. If it is too large to fit in the portfolio, a photograph is taken. If a play or dramatic reading is performed, it might be on videotape. Teachers, parents, and peers could be encouraged to write references regarding the student's demonstration of virtue, citing specific examples. Sometimes a checklist is included.

Because a portfolio is primarily **self-assessment**, it encourages students to take control of and assume responsibility for documenting their own character development. A portfolio is personal. It includes the items a student wishes to have in it. The format is open-ended, allowing for student choice and creativity.

Sometimes students decorate a box and include artifacts that depict their character. Objects like a sculpture, a keepsake, something from nature, or other three-dimensional things can be included.

Student Profile

Another assessment tool is a student profile, similar to the Individualized Education Plan (IEP).

Sample Student Profile

Core Value: Honesty			
Strengths	Contributed by student	Contributed by Teacher	Contributed by Parent
Strategies for improvement			

Guidelines for Writing a Character Profile

Trustworthiness

What does this word mean?

What kinds of things have you done to show that you are trustworthy?
    Give examples.

In what kinds of situations is it difficult for you to be trustworthy?

What are your goals in this area?

What do you plan to do to improve your trustworthiness?

Character Construct

A common construct for character includes moral knowing, moral feeling, and moral doing. Each of these can be measured. According to the *Eleven principles of effective character education"* (Lickona, Schaps, Lewis, undated), teachers can measure moral judgment, moral commitment, and self-reported moral behavior.

Moral Knowing

Question/Answer Tests

Teachers use short answer, true/false, matching, multiple choice, and essay tests to measure student knowledge in a specific area. These tests can be used for measuring vocabulary, knowledge of laws, governmental structure, and even students' ideas about what is correct behavior and what is not.

Here are examples of teacher-devised test items for measuring moral knowledge:

Short Answer

What does "trustworthy" mean?

List ways you can show trustworthiness in this class.

List places or situations in which trustworthiness is important.

List behaviors that would show a lack of trustworthiness.

Are you a trustworthy person? Why or why not? Give examples.

Describe an incident in a book, movie, current events, or real life in which someone was trustworthy.

What are some predictable results of being trustworthy? of not being trustworthy?

True or False

___ Classroom rules are suspended when the teacher leaves the room.

___ Turning in homework on time is an example of trustworthiness.

Multiple Choice

A student who was absent should:

___ a. not worry about what he/she missed.

___ b. find out from other students what he/she missed.

___ c. ask the teacher what he/she missed.

___ d. make an appointment with the teacher to make up assignments.

Essay

Write an essay on honesty: What is it? Why is it important? How can it be demonstrated?

Case Studies

When given a short vignette or case study, students state what they should do and why. Students explain how the problem should be solved. Card games like *Choices* present these kinds of moral cases for students to solve. Sometimes teachers write case studies based on situations that have arisen in the classroom. There might be an index card box and anyone can add cards throughout the year. Here is an example of a teacher-made case study:

You were sick to your stomach last night, so didn't do your homework. If you don't turn your work in, you will get a zero for the assignment. Your teacher said he doesn't accept excuses. Your friend was also sick, but she copied the answers from someone else. Should you do the same? Why or why not?

James Rest has developed a well-known, standardized test of moral reasoning called the Defining Issues Test (1973). It uses the case study approach and computerized scoring makes it relatively simple to both administer and obtain results.

Moral Feeling

The measurement of moral feeling, beliefs, and attitudes is a relatively new field. Self-report and projective measures are the main methods used. Assessment instruments include sentence completion, picture interpretation such as the Thematic Apperception Test, the Rorschach (ink blot), a checklist of statements with which participants agree or disagree, rating scales for simple statements, rank ordering of values, and journal entries. Krathwohl developed a taxonomy of affective skills where check marks are placed next to various feelings.

Here are some sample forms of affective assessment:
Sentence Completion (Students listen and complete the sentence orally.):
I believe honesty is...
Going to school makes me...
I wish everyone in the world would...

Thematic Apperception Type Test

Show the student magazine pictures of situations such as a fight or someone sick in bed. Ask the student to describe the picture. Use probes like, "Is he doing the right thing?" "What should she do?" "How does he feel?" "How does she feel?"

Self-Report Checklist *(Students check the statements which best describe themselves.)*

_____ I think honesty is important.

_____ Sometimes I lie if I think it won't hurt anyone.

Self-Report Rating Scale *(1= disagree; 5= agree)*

1. Honesty is important.   1   2   3   4   5
2. It is all right to lie if you won't get caught.   1   2   3   4   5

Rank Ordering *(Put a 1 next to what you believe is the most important. Continue to use numbers to rank the following items):*

_____ Honesty

_____ Caring about others

_____ Self-fulfillment

_____ Making a lot of money

_____ Getting good grades in school

Journal Entry

Write about a time when you were honest. Why were you honest? How did you feel? Do you think you did the right thing? Would you do the same thing again?

Whenever self-report is used, there is a question of truthfulness. Students may be eager to please the teacher or peers, and so they give an "acceptable" answer. They may be lacking in intra-personal skills. This would cause them to inaccurately report on themselves. Or, they may see the assessment as an invasion of privacy, forcing disclosure in an area where they are uncomfortable because it is highly personal.

Moral Doing

Measuring behavior is time consuming because it requires sustained periods of direct observation by trained observers. Ideally, observations take place in a naturalistic environment such as the classroom, home, or playground. The goal is to measure naturally occurring moral behavior.

Time Sampling

One way to measure moral behavior is to keep frequency counts of identified behaviors. The data are fairly objective, can be validated by another observer, and are usable for sophisticated statistical analysis. The observer records a tally next to each behavior whenever it is observed.

Here is a sample of the observational assessment using a frequency count which I used for my dissertation research.

Name of Child:	Date:	Time:	to	Age of child:
Area where observation took place:				
Helps				
Shares				
Comforts				
Displays affection				

The user makes a tally each time he or she sees the behaviors.

Event Sampling

Historically, teachers placed stars on a chart for each good deed or completed assignment. This is an event sampling. It is possible to measure accomplishments quickly by adding up the stars.

Who Does the Assessment and When?

I believe the best assessment is self-assessment. Glasser (1992) stated that each student needs to learn self-evaluation. Students are expected to hold themselves accountable for their own behavior and work. To help students assess themselves, the teacher asks, *"What did you do? Did you do the right thing? What should you have done? What should you do now?"* Before evaluating student work the teacher asks, *"Did you do your best work? Is this quality? What are its strengths and weaknesses?"* Glasser recommends that students be asked to put a Q on what they consider to be quality work. Sometimes teachers leave time at the end of the day for daily evaluation. In the planning process described in chapter 5 this is called recall: *review* and *evaluation*. It may be oral, using a class meeting format. It could be called the "Six O'clock News," in which each student describes his or her accomplishments of the day. Students could write in their journals or fill out a simple checklist.

Benjamin Franklin (Loren, 1994) practiced daily self-evaluation regarding the thirteen virtues he believed important. Each day he checked himself, and made a mark if he needed to improve. He kept charts to show his improvement or decline in each of thirteen virtues.

Ben Franklin's Checklist

Virtue	Sun	Mon	Tue	Wed	Thur	Fri	Sat
Temperance							
Silence							
Order							
Resolution							
Frugality							
Industry							
Sincerity							
Justice							
Chastity							
Humility							
Tranquillity							
Cleanliness							
Moderation							

Sometimes more than one person evaluates a student. There might be an assessment team made up of the student, parents, teachers, and peers. Often there are many educators and para-professionals who work with the same students. The student may choose the team, or it may be limited to the people who work most closely with the student. Each member of the team can perform an independent character evaluation, then meet to compare ratings. These kinds of in-depth evaluations are usually performed once a semester or year at a parent conference.

Classroom Assessment

Sometimes teachers want to know how the class is doing as a whole and whether teaching strategies are effective. The teacher might ask, "What did you think of this assignment? What did you learn from it? What suggestions do you have for next year's class when they do this assignment?" In some of my college classes, students use an index card to summarize and evaluate during the last five minutes of the class period. They also fill out an evaluation at the end of each semester.

Students may be asked to circle the numbers of the items that are true:
1. I like my class.
2. My teacher likes me.
3. When I have a problem, other students help me.
4. I am learning about respect and responsibility in this class.
5. The students in this class don't really care about each other.

Here is another form of class assessment:

☺ =Yes   ☹ =No
○ I am learning about honesty in school.
○ I am more honest now than I was last year.
○ I like our character education program.
○ My teacher talks about honesty.
○ I want to be honest.

There are other tools for evaluating the class. Some teachers ask a peer to come in and observe. Questionnaires can be sent to parents. A portfolio with pictures, newsletters, and other items may show class work in the area of character education. A **class profile** which is filled out by the teacher or class, might look like this:

Core Value: Responsibility

Action Do Now	Action Could Do	Action Plan	Who is in charge & involved	Target Date	Date Accomplished

I have developed a classroom teacher's assessment kit for identifying comprehensive character building classrooms. It includes criteria based on the outline of this book. They are divided into six categories: moral leadership, moral climate, moral community, moral correction, moral curriculum, and common projects. These are referred to as the LC5 model. The kit also contains an assessment tool, "Comprehensive character building classroom assessment instrument" (or CBCI), a questionnaire for parents, a questionnaire for students, and a suggested method of assessment which includes observations, interviews, and a team meeting. Having served as a validator for the National Academy of Early Childhood Programs, and a national representative for the Council for Early Childhood Professional Recognition, I have seen and participated in well designed classroom and classroom teacher assessments. The same methods can be applied in assessing the comprehensive character building classroom.

Assessment Of Character Education

Summary

Character and character education in the classroom can be measured using a variety of assessment tools. Assessment includes three components: a) selecting criteria; b) designing a tool or instrument by which to measure the criteria; c) deciding on methodology: who, where, when, and how. Assessment is the primary vehicle for validating one's efforts and planning future activities. Assessment of character and character education may be accomplished through checklists, rating scales, anecdotal entries, portfolios, and profiles.

In order to measure character, one must measure moral knowledge, moral beliefs, and moral behavior. Teachers have devised tests such as short answer, true/false, multiple choice, essays, and case studies for measuring moral knowledge. Moral feelings and beliefs are usually measured through sentence completion, a thematic apperception type test, rating scales, and rank ordering. Moral behavior is measured through time or event sampling or self report.

In addition to assessment of individuals, the program itself can be assessed by the teacher, students, parents, and an outside observer.

Exercise

1. *Design an assessment tool based on the universal values you have chosen to promote. Pilot it with students and parents.*
2. *Use the assessment tool designed by the author for measuring the comprehensive character-building classroom.*

References

American Psychological Association. (1995). *Publication manual.* (4th ed.). Washington, D.C.: American Psychological Association.

Appleton's school reader: Introduction for fourth grade. 1884. American Book Co.

Aristotle. (1943). *Politics.* L. R. Loomis (Ed.). Roslyn, N.Y.: Walter J. Black, Inc.

Baker, M. (1989). *Book A-1 What would you do?* Pacific Grove, CA: Midwest Publications.

Baker, M. (1989). *Book B-1 What would you do?* Pacific Grove, CA: Critical Thinking Press and Software.

Baltimore County Public Schools. (1983). "1984 and beyond. A reaffirmation of values." A report of the task force on values education and ethical behavior of the Baltimore County public schools. Baltimore County Public Schools, Towson, MD 21204.

Bandura, A. (1971). *Social learning theory.* New York: General Learning Press.

Baumrind, D. (1971). Current patterns of parental authority. *Developmental Psychology, 4,* 1-103.

Bedford School District. (1995). *Parent Handbook.* Bedford School Department, 150 County Road, Bedford, N.H. 03110.

Beedy, J. (1996). *Personal learning using sports.* PLUS Institute PO Box 219, New Hampton, N.H. 03256. (603)744-5401; (603)744-3769 fax.

Bennett, W. (1993). *The book of virtues.* New York: Simon & Schuster.

Bennett, W. (1995). *The moral compass.* New York: Simon & Schuster.

Bill of Rights for Children. Presented to the National Education Association Representative Assembly, July 4, 1991.

Bodine, R., Crawford, D. & Schrumpf, F. (1994). *Creating the peaceable school a comprehensive program for teaching conflict resolution.* Champaign, IL: Research Press.

Boston University. (1993). *The art of loving well: A character education curriculum for today's teenagers.* Boston, MA: Boston University.

Brabeck, M. (Ed.) (1989). *Who cares?* New York: Praeger.

Business and Education. (1991). "What should they be able to do?" Education report of the Business and Industry Association of New Hampshire, 122 North Main Street, Concord, N.H. 03301; (800)540-5388; (603)224-2872, fax.

Camp, B. and Bash, M. (1985). *Think aloud: Increasing social and cognitive skills— A problem-solving program for children. Champaign, IL: Research Press.*

Campbell, R. (1981). *How to really love your teenager.* Wheaton, IL: Victor Books.

Canter, L. & Canter, M. (1992). *Assertive discipline.* CA: Lee Canter Associates.

Charney, R. (1992). *Teaching children to care.* Greenfield, MA: Northeast Foundation.

Childcraft: The how and why library. (1982) Chicago: World Book, Inc.

Children's Defense Fund. *State of America's children yearbook 1996.* 25 E. Street NW, Washington, D.C. 20001. (202)628-8787.

Coles, R. (1986). *The moral life of children.* Boston: Houghton Mifflin Co.

Coles, R. (1989). *The call of stories.* Boston: Houghton Mifflin Co.

Cozby, P., Worden, P. & Kee, D. (1989). *Research methods in human development.* CA: Mayfield Publishing Company.

Crary, E. (1984). *Kids can cooperate.* Seattle, WA: Parenting Press, Inc.

Damon, W. (1988). *The moral child: Nurturing children's natural moral growth.* New York: Macmillan.

Dewey, J. (1954). *Moral principles in education.* New York: Philosophical Library.

Dishon, D. & O'Leary, P. (1994). *A guidebook for cooperative learning* (2nd ed.). Holmes Beach, FL: Learning Publications, Inc.

Dobson, J. (1992). *The new dare to discipline.* Wheaton, IL: Tyndale.

Dreikurs, R. & Grey, L. (1968). *A new approach to discipline: Logical consequences.* New York: Hawthorne Books.

Dreikurs, R. (1968). *Psychology in the classroom: A manual for teachers* (2nd ed.). New York: Harper & Row.

Drew, N. (1987). *Learning the skills of peacemaking: An activity guide for elementary-age children on communicating, cooperating, resolving conflict.* Rolling Hills Estates, CA: Jalmar Press.

Dreyer, S. (1994). *The bookfinder.* Circle Pines, MN: American Guidance Service, Inc.

Egan, K. (1986). *Teaching as storytelling.* Chicago: University of Chicago Press.

Eisenberg, N. & Miller, T. (1987). The relation of empathy to prosocial and related behaviors. *Psychological Bulletin, 17,* 7 73-782.

Erikson, E. (1950). *Childhood and society.* New York: Norton.

Ethics Resource Center. (1994). *The teaching of ethics.* Ethics Resource Center, Inc., 1120 G St., NW, Ste. 200, Washington, D.C. 20005.

Evans, K. (undated). Union County child care's ethical communication principles. Union County Child Care & Learning Center, 140 N. Second St., Lewisburg, PA 17837.

Evertson, C., Emmer, E., Clements, B., Sanford, J. & Worsham, M. (1989). *Classroom management for elementary teachers.* NJ: Prentice Hall.

Feeney, S. & Kipnis, K. (1992). Code of ethical conduct. National Association for the Education of Young Children, 1509 16th Street NW, Washington, D.C. 20036. (800)424-2460.

Fraiberg, S. (1959) *The magic years.* New York: Charles Scribner & Sons.

Franklin, B. *Autobiography.*

Freed, A. & Freed, M. ((1983). *TA for kids.* Rolling Hills Estates, CA: Jalmar Press.

Geough, R. (1996). *Character is everything: Promoting ethical excellence in sports.* New York: Harcourt Brace.

Gilligan, C. (1982). *In a different voice: Psychological theory and women's development.* Cambridge, MA: Harvard University Press.

Ginott, H. (1972). *Between teacher and child.* New York: Macmillan Publishing Company, Inc.

Glasser, W. (1969). *Schools without failure.* New York: Harper & Collins.

Glasser, W. (1975). *Reality therapy.* New York: Harper & Row.

Glasser, W. (1985). *Control theory in the classroom.* New York: Harper & Row.

Glasser, W. (1992). *The quality school.* New York: HarperCollins Publishers.

Glasser, W. (1993). *The quality school teacher.* New York: HarperCollins Publishers.

Gordon, T. (1974). *Teacher effectiveness training.* New York: Peter H. Wyden Publishers.

Greer, C. & Kohl, H. (Ed.). (1995). *A call to character*. New York: HarperCollins Publishers.

Harmin, M. (1990). How to plan a program for moral education. Washington, D.C.: Association for Supervision and Curriculum Development.

Hartshorne, H. & May, M. (1928). *Studies in the nature of character. 1. Studies in deceit*. New York: Macmillan.

Hartshorne, H. & May, M. (1930). *Studies in the nature of character, 3. Studies in the organization of character*. New York: Macmillan.

Hauerwas, S. (1983). *The peaceable kingdom*. Notre Dame, IN: University of Notre Dame Press.

Hoffman, M. (1963). Parent discipline and the child's consideration for others. *Child Development, 31*, 90-126.

Hoffman, M. (1975). Altruistic behavior and the parent-child relationship. *Journal of Personality and Social Review, 3*(3), 274-291.

Hohmann, M., Banet, B., & Weikart, D. (1979). *Young children in action*. Ypsilanti MI: The High/Scope Press.

Huffman, H. (1994). *A character education program*. Alexandria, VA: Association for Supervision and Curriculum Development.

Hung, G. (1989). *Honey for a child's heart* (3rd ed.). Grand Rapids, MI: Zondervan.

Johnson, J., Collins, H., Dupuis, V., Johansen, J. (1991). *Introduction to the foundations of American education*. Boston: Allyn and Bacon.

Jones, F. (1987). *Positive classroom discipline*. New York: Macmillan-Hill Book Company.

Josephson, M. (1991). Aspen Declaration. Character Counts! Coalition, Josephson Institute of Ethics, 4640 Admiralty Way, Suite 1001, Marina del Rey, CA 90292; (310)306-1868; (310)827-1864 fax; cc@jethics.org.

Kant, I. In Churton, A. (trans.), *Kant on education*. London: Kegan, Paul, Trench, Trubner. (Original work published in 1899).

Kennedy, J. (1994). *Character and destiny*. Grand Rapids, MI: Zondervan.

Kidder, R. (1995). *How good people make tough choices*. New York: A Fireside Book.

Kilpatrick, W., Wolfe, G. & S. (1994). *Books that build character*. New York: Simon & Schuster.

Kilpatrick, W. (1986). The use of literature in character formation. In *Content, character and choice: Public policy and research implications*. Washington, D.C.: National Council on Educational Research. (pp. 85-92).

Kilpatrick, W. (1992). *Why Johnny can't tell right from wrong*. New York: Simon & Schuster.

Kohlberg, L. (1981). *Essays on moral development, v. 1 The philosophy of moral development*. San Francisco: Harper & Row.

Kohn, A. (1993). *Punished by rewards*. Boston: Houghton Mifflin Co.

Kounin, J. (1997). By C. Edwards. *Classroom discipline & management* (2nd ed.). Columbus, OH: Merrill.

Kreidler, W. (1984). *Creative conflict resolution*. Glenview, IL: Scott, Foresman and Company.

Lanier, J., & Cusick, P. (1985). The educator's oath. *Phi Delta Kappan*, June. 711-712.

Levin, D. (1994). *Teaching young children in violent times: A preschool-grade 3 violence prevention and conflict resolution guide*. Cambridge, MA: Educators for Social Responsibility.

Lewis, C. S. (1947). *The abolition of man*. New York: Macmillan.

Lickona, T. (Ed.). (1975). *Moral development and behavior*. New York: Holt, Rinehart and Winston.

Lickona, T. (1992). *Educating for character: How our schools can teach respect and responsibility*. New York: Bantam Books.

Lickona, T. (1994). *Raising good children*. New York: Bantam.

Lipson, G. & Lipson, E. (1988). *Everyday law for young citizens*. Carthage, IL: Good Apple, Inc.

Loren, M. (1994). *What counts*. Independence, MO: Overland Park Press.

MacIntyre, A. (1984). *After virtue*. Notre Dame, IN: University of Notre Dame Press.

Mann, H. (1846). *Life and works of Horace Mann*. Boston: Liam Shepherd.

Mannix, D. (1989). *Be a better student*. West Nyack, NY: Center for Applied Research in Education.

Martens, R. (1981). *Kid sports and moral development*. CA: Wadsworth.

Martin, G. & Pear, J. (1996). *Behavior modification*. (5th ed.). Upper Saddle River, NJ: Prentice Hall.

McCaslin, N. (1990). *Creative drama in the classroom.* (5th ed.). New York: Longman.

Mcmillan, J. & Schumacker, S. (1984). *Research in education.* Boston: Little, Brown & Co.

Meichenbaum, D. (1977). *Cognitive behavior modification: An integrative approach.* New York: Plenum.

Morality. (1992). November. *World Monitor.*

National Education Association. (1974). Code of Ethics. Washington, D.C.: National Education Association.

New Hampshire Department of Education. (1995). *K-12 science curriculum framework.* Department of Education, 101 Pleasant Street, Concord, N.H. 03301. (603)271-3743.

Noddings, N. (1984). *Caring: A feminine approach to ethics & moral education.* Berkeley: University of California Press.

Notre Dame College Student Handbook. 1995-1996. Notre Dame College, 2321 Elm Street, Manchester, N.H. 03104.

Nucci, L. (Ed.) (1989). *Moral development and character education.* Berkeley, CA: McCrutcheon Publishing Corporation.

Oliner, S. & Oliner, P. (1988). *The altruistic person.* New York: Free Press.

Parr, S. (1982). *The moral of the story.* New York: Teachers College Press.

Phi Alpha Delta Public Service Center. (1994). *Respect reflect resolve: Ten anti-violence lessons for use in middle and high school.* Washington, D.C.: Phi Alpha Delta Public Service Center.

Piaget, J. (1965). *The moral judgment of the child.* (M. Gabain, Trans.) New York: Free Press.

Plato (1942). *Apology.* (B. Jowett, Trans.) Roslyn, N.Y: Walter J. Black, Inc.

Plato (1942). *Republic.* (B. Jowett, Trans.) Roslyn, N.Y.: Walter J. Black, Inc.

Pritchard, I. (1988). *Moral education and character.* U.S. Department of Education: Office of Educational Research and Improvement.

Prutzman, P., Stern, L., Burger, M. & Godenhamer, G. (1988). *The friendly classroom for a small planet: Children's creative response to conflict program.* Philadelphia: New Society Publishers.

Raths, L., Harmin, M. & Simon, S. (1966). *Values and teaching*. Columbus, OH: Charles E. Merrill Publishing Co.

Rest, J. (1973). Patterns of preference and comprehension in moral judgment. *Journal of Personality. 41*. 86-109.

Rieff, P. (1959). *Freud: The mind of the moralist*. New York: Doubleday.

Robert's rules of order. (1907). New York: Bell Publishing Company.

Ryan, K. and Cooper, J. (1988). *Those who can, teach*. (5th ed.). Boston: Houghton Mifflin Co.

Ryan, K. (1986). The new moral education. *Phi Delta Kappan*. November, 228-233.

Salzman, M. & Reisgies, T. (1991). *150 ways teens can make a difference*. Princeton, N.J.: Peterson's Guide.

Santrock, J., & Yussen, S. (1988). *Child Development*. (4th ed.). Dubuque, IA: Wm. C. Brown Publishers.

Shapiro, S. (1994). Memo to Clinton. *Tikkun 9*(3) 92.

Schmidt, F., Friedman, A. & Marvel, J. (1992). *Mediation for kids*. Miami Beach, FL: Grace Contrino Abrams Peace Education Foundation.

Schulman, M. (1995). *Schools as moral communities*. New York: Jewish Foundation for Christian Rescuers.

Schultz, T., Wright, K., & Schleifer, M. (1986). Assignment of moral responsibility and punishment. *Child Development, 57*, 177-184.

Shure, M. & Spivack, G. (1974). *The preschool interpersonal problem solving test manual*. Philadelphia: Hahnemann Medical College and Hospital.

Shure, M. & Spivack, G. (1988). *The what happens next game test manual*. Philadelphia: Hahnemann University.

Shure, M. (1989). *Interpersonal cognitive problem solving: A mental health program for kindergarten and first grade children*. Philadelphia: Hahnemann University.

Shure, M. (1992). *I can problem solve: An interpersonal cognitive problem-solving program intermediate elementary grades*. Champaign IL: Research Press.

Smith, C. (1993). *The peaceful classroom: 162 easy activities to teach preschoolers compassion and cooperation*. Mount Rainier, MD: Gryphon House.

Stanton, J. In *New York Nursery Education News* (1954) Winter.

Thompson, J. (1995). *Positive coaching: Building character and self-esteem through sports*. Portola Valley, CA: Warde Publishers.

Tomlinson, P. & Quinton, M. (1986). *Values across the curriculum.* Philadelphia: Falmer Press.

Trimmer, J. (1994) *A guide to MLA documentation* (3rd ed.) Boston: Houghton Mifflin.

Unell, B. & Wyckoff, J. (1995). *Twenty teachable virtues.* New York: Perigee Book.

Urban, H. (1992). *Life's greatest lessons.* Nashville, TN: Thomas Nelson Publishers.

Veroff, J., & Veroff, J. (1980). *Social incentives: A life-span developmental approach.* San Diego, CA: Academie Press.

Vincent, P. (1994). *Developing character in students.* Chapel Hill, N.C.: New View Publications.

Vincent, P. (Ed.) (1996). *Promising practices in character education.* Chapel Hill, N.C.: Character Development Group.

Vygotsky, L. (1934). *Thought and language.* Cambridge, MA: M.I.T. Press.

Wanner, S. (1994). *On with the story: Adolescents learning through narrative.* Portsmouth, N.H.: Heinemann.

Webster's New Collegiate Dictionary (1980). Boston, MA: G. & C. Merriam Company.

Wezeman, P. (1990). *Peacemaking creatively through the arts.* Prescott, AZ: Educational Ministries.

Whiting, L., & Whiting, B. (1975). *Children of six cultures.* Cambridge, MA: Harvard University Press.

Wichert, S. (1989). *Keeping the peace: Practicing cooperation and conflict resolution with preschoolers.* Philadelphia: New Society Publishers.

Wilson, E. (1987). *Books children love.* Westchester, IL: Crossway Book.

Wynne, E. & Ryan, K. (1993). *Reclaiming our schools.* New York: Merrill.

Wynne, E. (1986). The great tradition in education: Transmitting moral values. *Educational Leadership*, December 1985/January 1986, 73-81.

Zahn-Waxler, C. & Radkey-Yarrow, M. (1979). Child rearing and children's prosocial initiations toward victims of distress. *Child Development, 50,* 319-330.

Zlotkowski, E. (1995). Service-Learning Project: A Presentation at Keene State College. Bentley College, 175 Forest St., Waltham, MA 02154; (617)891-1170; fax: (617)891-2896; ezlotkowski@bentley.edu.

Movies

Character Education: Restoring Respect and Responsibility in our Schools. National Professional Resources, Inc., 25 South Regent Street, Port Chester, N.Y. 10573; (800)453-7461.

Commitment to Character. CEP, 809 Franklin St., Alexandria, VA 22314; (800)988-8081.

For Goodness Sake. United Learning, 6633 West Howard St., P.O. Box 48718, Niles, IL 60714.

Why Dick and Jane lie, cheat and steal. Character Education Institute, 8918 Tesoro Drive, Suite 575, San Antonio, TX 78217.

Sunburst Communications, 39 Washington Ave., P.O. Box 40, Pleasantville, N.Y. 10570; (800)431-1934; (914)769-2109 fax.

Thought, Word, and Deed: Teaching character through respect and responsibility—for self, others and society. State Farm Insurance, Public Affairs Dept., One State Farm Plaza, Bloomington, IL 61710.

Games

LifeStories. (1989). FNDI Ltd. Partnership, Golden Valley, MN 55427. Distributed by Standard Publishing, Cincinnati, OH 45231.

Smart Choices. Trend Enterprises, Inc., St. Paul, MN 55164.

Kid's Choices. Rainfall, Grand Rapids, MI 49507.

Teen Choices. Rainfall, Grand Rapids, MI 49507.

Educational Programs and Resource Centers

Center for Civic Education, 5146 Douglas Fir Road, Calabasas, CA 91302; (800)350-4223; (818)591-9330 fax.

Center for Learning, B21590 Center Ridge Road, Rocky River, OH 44116. (216)331-1401; (216)331-5414 fax.

Center for the 4th and 5th Rs, State University of New York at Cortland, P.O. Box 2000, Cortland, N.Y. 13045; (607)753-2455; (607)753-5980 fax

Center for the Advancement of Ethics and Character, School of Education, Boston University, 605 Commonwealth Ave., Boston, MA 02215.

Character Education Institute, 8918 Tesoro Drive, Suite 575, San Antonio, TX 78217.

Character Education Partnership, 809 Franklin St., Alexandria, VA 22314; (800)988-8081; (703)739-4967 fax.

Communitarian Network, 2130 H Street NW, Suite 714J, Washington, D.C. 20052; (202)994-7997; (202)994-1606 fax; comnet@unix1.circ.gwu.edu.

Community of Caring, 1325 G Street NW, Suite 500, Washington, D.C. 20005; (202)393-1250; (202)824-0200 fax.

Developmental Studies Center, 2000 Embarcadero, Suite 305, Oakland, CA 94606; (510)533-0213; (510)464-3670 fax.

Ethics Resource Center, Education Department, 1120 G Street NW, Suite 200, Washington, D.C. 20005; (800)777-1285.

Facing History and Ourselves National Foundation, Inc., 16 Hurd Road, Brookline, MA 02146-6919; (617)232-1595; (617)232-0281 fax.

Giraffe Project, P.O. Box 759, Langley, WA 98260; (360)221-7989.

Good Citizenship and Courtesy Program, Anne Lyons, 705 E. Burnsville Pkwy., Burnsville, MN 55337.

Heartwood Institute, 425 N. Craig St., Suite 302, Pittsburg, PA 15213; (412)688-8570; (412)688-8552 fax.

Institute for Global Ethics, P.O. Box 563, Camden, ME 04843. (207)236-6658; (207)236-4014 fax.

Jefferson Center for Character Education, 2700 East Foothill Blvd., Suite 302, Pasadena, CA 91107; (818)792-8130; (818)792-8364 fax.

Responsive Classroom, Northeast Foundation for Children, 71 Montague City Road, Greenfield, MA 01301; (800)360-NEFC.

Personal Responsibility Education Process, The Network for Educational Development, 13157 Olive Spur Road, St. Louis, MO 63141; (314)576-3535.

School for Ethical Education, 1000 Lafayette Boulevard, Bridgeport, CT 06604; (203)330-5052; (203)330-5001 fax.

Teaching Tolerance, 400 Washington Avenue, Montgomery, AL 36104; (205)264-0286; (205)264-3121 fax.

The National Institute of Ethics, 220 Live Oaks Blvd., Building 2, Casselberry, FL 32707; (407)-339-0322; (407)339-7139 fax.

Wee Deliver, Office of Literacy, U.S. Postal Service, 470 L'Enfant Plaza SW, Room 4102E, Washington, D.C. 20260.

Young People's Press, Inc., 1731 Kettner Blvd., San Diego, CA 92101.

Appendix

Planning Checklist

Checklist for implementing planning (adapted from Hohmann, Banet, & Weikart, (1979):

GOAL SETTING
___1. Students are encouraged to share their visions and ideals.
___2. Students generate lists of character traits they wish to develop.
___3. Students set goals for their own development.

PLANNING
4. At the beginning of the year, the teacher gets students ready to start the planning process by helping them:
___a. learn what materials and equipment are available.
___b. learn the names of the work areas.
___c. learn the names of other people.
___d. begin to make choices.
___e. learn to use planning forms.
___5. Planning occurs each day at the same time and place.
___6. Students can see the resources in the room while planning.
___7. There is a planning board, file folder, or some other way to keep track of students' plans.
___8. Each student shares his or her plan with the teacher and/or peers.
___9. The teacher points out new materials or special activities which students may want to include in their plans.
10. The teacher talks with each student in turn:
___a. asking the student what he or she would like to do.
___b. giving the student time to respond.
___c. acknowledging the choice or plan the student makes.
___d. helping the student expand his/her plan.
___e. giving suggestions if the student can't think of anything.
___f. reminding the student of something he or she began yesterday, if such is the case.
___g. recording or examining records of the student's plan.

11. Depending on the students' needs, the teacher helps students:

___a. vary their plans from day to day.

___b. make a series of connected plans.

___c. make realistic plans.

___d. make plans with others.

12. Each student indicates what he or she is going to do during work time either by:

___a. naming an area, resources, or student to work with.

___b. describing the plan through telling, writing, or drawing.

___13. Time is spent wisely during and after planning.

___14. The teacher watches to see which students need assistance to get started on their plans.

___15. The teacher helps students who need assistance with their plans as soon as every student has made a plan and has started working.

WORKING

___16. Students have time (30–90 minutes) to carry out their plans and make new ones when finished.

___17. Each student is actively involved with the materials he/she has chosen.

___18. Students get their own materials.

___19. Each student works on his/her plan.

___20. Students converse intermittently with the teacher or other students about what they are doing.

___21. Each student attempts to solve problems as they come up or seeks assistance.

___22. Students clean up their own materials when they're finished with them unless another student is using them or will add to what was done.

___23. Each student makes a new plan when the initial plan is finished.

___24. The teacher tries to keep in mind what is happening in the whole room, moving from student to student throughout work time.

_____25. The teacher assists students who:
  a. need help getting started on their plans.
  b. ask for help as they are working.
  c. don't seem to know what to do next.
  d. are making new plans.

_____26. The teacher works with each student at his/her own level.

_____27. The teacher talks with students about what they are doing.

_____28. The teacher recognizes and supports students' work by doing one or more of the following:
  a. describing what a student seems to be doing.
  b. asking a student to tell what he/she is doing.
  c. trying out a student's ideas.
  d. helping students gather materials for their ideas.
  e. having a student show another student what he/she is doing.
  f. helping students use problem solving strategies.

_____29. The teacher helps students extend their plans and ideas by doing one or more of the following:
  a. helping students find additional materials.
  b. asking students open-ended questions to help them see what they could do next with their plans.
  c. helping students relate their work to someone else's.
  d. helping students save or represent what they have done.
  e. planning experiences and/or field trips relating to students' work.
  f. helping each student extend his/her plan along the student's own interests and at the student's own pace.
  g. taking cues from students about when their plans are complete.

30. The teacher helps students deal with work time conflicts by doing one or more of the following:
  _____a. ignoring small conflicts and letting students work them out themselves.
  _____b. restructuring the environment so that more materials and space are available, anticipating problems before they develop.

____c. using calming and cool-down strategies when students are losing emotional control.

____d. offering choices to students.

____e. using negotiation strategies (problem solving).

____f. bringing problems to the whole class to solve.

____g. asking other students to help students solve the conflicts.

____h. offering suggestions of alternative strategies.

____31. The teacher records observations of students throughout work time.

____32. The teacher helps students recall and evaluate during work time as plans are completed.

REPRESENT

____33. When students complete a plan, the teacher encourages representation through one of the following:

telling (oral language), writing, drawing, making a model, photography, role play, audio tape recording, videotaping.

____34. The teacher encourages and supports students' representational activities by:

a. encouraging students to represent in a variety of two- and three-dimensional media.

c. talking with students about their representations.

d. encouraging students to make their own books, songs, and stories.

e. providing real experiences directly related to things students are attempting to represent.

f. providing opportunities for students to interpret other people's representations.

g. following up real experiences with opportunities to represent the experience.

CLEAN UP

___35. Students do most of the clean up work, returning materials to their proper places.

___36. The teacher alerts students to clean up toward the end of work time (5-minute warning) and then uses a consistent signal to mark the beginning of clean-up time.

___37. The teacher explains the reasons for cleaning up.

___38. The teacher helps students name what materials they're going to put away.

___39. The teacher talks with students about the kinds of things they are putting away.

___40. The teacher works along with the students at clean-up time.

___41. The teacher makes up clean-up games based on what the students are doing and what they enjoy.

___42. The teacher designates a place where students gather as they finish cleaning up.

___43. The teacher calls group meetings to assess the progress and problems of clean up on difficult days.

___44. The teacher gives a student having difficulty with cleaning up a choice of tasks, then monitors finishing the chosen task.

RECALL TIME and EVALUATION

___45. Students talk about their work. Emphasis is NOT put on products to be displayed, but on the plan and work done.

___46. All students participate in recall, not just those who made a product.

___47. The teacher listens and supports students as they recall what they did.

___48. The teacher experiments with a variety of ways to make recall time interesting to students (possibly small groups or individually).

___49. The teacher encourages students to evaluate their efforts.

Checklist for Problem Solving

____Teacher poses thinking questions.

____Students are given time to think after questions are posed.

____Students predict.

____Students test their hypotheses.

____Students evaluate their predictions.

____Students experiment.

____Teacher encourages students to solve their own problems.

____At group time, students are involved in decision making.

____The teacher encourages students to resolve their own crises.

____When students have problems, they try to solve them before asking for help.

____Students seem to take pleasure in solving problems.

____The teacher encourages students to assume responsibility for their own actions.

____The teacher brings up problems for students to discuss at large group time.

____Teacher uses problem solving vocabulary such as "problem," "solutions," "alternative solutions," "what would happen?" "ideas."

____Teacher focuses on the process of decision making rather than on quick, easy adult solutions. Emphasis is on logical thinking.

____Teacher focuses on student thinking by asking probing questions such as "tell me more."

____Teacher encourages more than one solution (at least three).

____Teacher encourages students to reflect on their own thinking and verbalize it by asking "Tell me how you solved that," etc.

____Teacher is a mentor, stimulating student initiative.

____The teacher employs guided problem-solving strategies when a crisis arises.

A Unit on Character

Character Trait:_____ Month:_____

Reading (books, stories, poems, plays)

_____

Writing (journal entries, story starters, poems, acrostics, riddles)

_____

Language (speeches, skits, plays, puppetry, charades)

_____

Spelling and vocabulary_____

Social Studies (examples from history, current issues)

_____

Math and Science (examples from history, current issues, attitudes, methods of teaching)

_____

Art (art appreciation, drawings, paintings, sculpture, posters, bumper stickers, murals, t-shirts, mobiles, collages, cartoon strips, coat of arms, banner, "stained glass window," play dough)

_____

Music (music appreciation, songs, musical compositions, creative song writing, and dance)

_____

Physical Education (sportsmanship, study of athletes)

_____

Library (reference and research)

_____

Methods of Teaching Character

Choose one trait:_____

1. Find heroes and heroines who exhibited this trait.
2. Find stories which demonstrate this trait (or its lack).
3. Study historical people who showed this trait.
4. Discuss newspaper articles in which this trait is shown.
5. Write an essay or position paper together.
6. Write a fable where the moral of the story is to show this trait.
7. Use puppets to put on a skit about this trait.
8. Use cross-age tutoring.
9. Have a fund-raiser or drive to help others.
10. Do community service.
11. Perform a school job.
12. Tell a story about this trait.
13. Write a poem.
14. Make an acrostic using this trait.
15. Make up a commercial about this trait.
16. Look this trait up in the dictionary.
17. Write a song about this trait. You may use a familiar tune.
18. Make a banner about this trait.
19. Make a poster promoting this trait.
20. Write a motto about this trait. Write it as graffiti.
21. Give public compliments to people who show this trait.
22. Send "character grams" to people who show this trait.
23. Earn points by showing this trait.
24. Send notes to people who showed this trait (real people living today or people in the past).
25. Memorize a poem about this trait. Use it as a "mantra."
26. Memorize mottos about this trait.
27. Use mottos as morals to illustrate a story about this trait.
28. Talk about the trait: what it means, how it is shown in everyday life, how it is not shown.

29. Look for opportunities to demonstrate this trait. List possibilities together. Keep track of who followed through.

30. Use role play for tough situations. Act out how the trait might or might not be shown.

31. Make up a cheer promoting this trait.

32. Decorate t-shirts, hats, and pins that promote this trait. Wear them.

33. Demonstrate the trait throughout the day.

34. Explain a poem which refers to this trait.

35. Design a cartoon series about this trait.

36. Draw a picture of someone showing this trait.

37. Use the computer to print this trait in different type faces.

38. Make a list of the ways you show the trait this week.

39. Make a mural depicting this trait in action.